Birthday Cakes

Birthday Cakes

Exciting designs with full
step-by-step instructions

Sylvia Coward
&
Shelley Birnie

NEW
HOLLAND

First published in the UK in 1994 by
New Holland (Publishers) Ltd
37 Connaught Street, London W2 2AZ

ISBN 1 85368 332 9 (hbk)
ISBN 1 85368 292 6 (pbk)

Editor Alison Leach
Designer Carole Perks
Photography by Tim Frowd and Hilda Kwan
Illustrations by Sue Thompson, Gina Daniel and Stuart Perry
Typeset by Ace Filmsetting Ltd, Frome, Somerset
Printed and bound in Malaysia

Contents

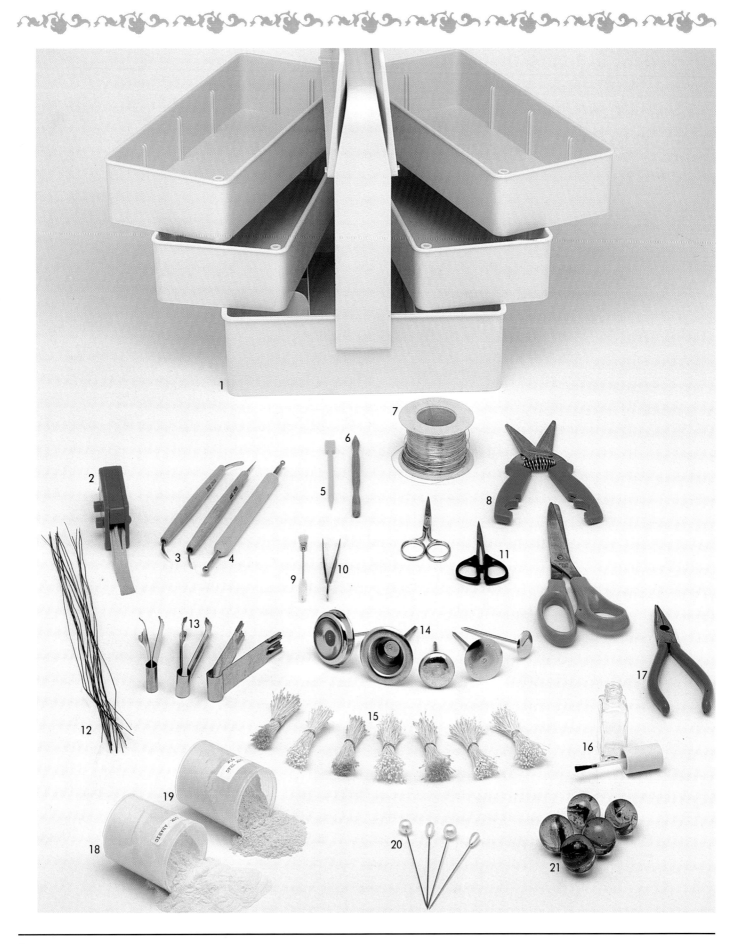

Tools and Equipment

There are certain basic tools, equipment and special ingredients which are essential for the various cake decorating techniques but numerous items can be added for the creation of different effects. The equipment shown here is by no means all that is available but it generally covers items used for the cakes and designs that are featured in this book.

Although it is an advantage to have all the right tools and equipment available, you may not always have access to them. You may, therefore, find items around the house which can be used most successfully.

Auger tool: This is a most useful tool which has many uses including hollowing small flowers.

Ball tools: Various sizes of ball tools are used for modelling and moulding flowers and figures.

Brushes: A selection of good quality paintbrushes in various sizes is essential for creating special effects.

Cocoa butter: This is mixed with cocoa powder and used in the *Cocoa Painting* technique described on page 28.

Container for egg white: A new and unused nail polish bottle and brush is most suitable for storing and applying egg white.

Crimpers: Available in a wide variety of shapes, these are used to create patterns on cakes by pinching the sugarpaste together.

Florist and tinned copper fuse wire: Florist or fuse wire is inserted into moulded flowers to facilitate the making up of sprays. The sprays are then attached to the cake with royal icing. The wire stems should never be inserted directly into the cake.

Florist tape: This is usually available in white, brown, light and dark green and is used for taping the wires for moulded flowers.

Flower cutters: Numerous metal and plastic cutters are available for making the different flowers.

Flower formers: These are the various plastic and wooden shapes used in the making of different moulded flowers.

Flower nails: A variety of flower nails is available; the one most commonly used consists of a flat metal or plastic disc on a spike and is used for piped royal icing flowers.

Flower stand/holder: I developed this wooden flower stand to facilitate the drying and storing of small moulded flowers.

Flower or leaf veiners: Rubber or plastic shapes that are pressed on to modelling paste to create veining on flowers and leaves.

Frill rulers: Scalloped cutters of different lengths, these are used for cutting modelling paste or pastillage to create a frilled or scalloped edge.

Gum Arabic: This can be used to glaze flowers to create a porcelain effect as well as to make edible glitter (see page 15).

Gum tragacanth: Available from specialist cake decorating shops and pharmacies, this powder is added to create the modelling paste used for making moulded flowers. It gives elasticity and is a drying agent.

Hobby or icing knife: A small knife is needed for certain types of work to cut modelling paste or pastillage.

Icing bags: For those who prefer not to use paper cones for piping, a nylon icing bag is preferable to the rigid syringe type.

Lifters: These are made from two pieces of thin board and are used for lifting the marzipan and sugarpaste on to the cake.

Manicure tool: Usually found in a manicure set, this tool is used successfully to create the features of various kinds of animals.

Moulds: These plastic or plaster moulds can be filled with sugar, chocolate or modelling paste. Certain moulds are available for creating figures.

Nozzles: See Tubes.

Painting knife: This is available from art shops and is used for lifting petals, leaves, and so on.

Palette: A small plastic artist's palette with little hollows is useful for mixing colours with water or cornflour and for mixing cocoa powder with cocoa butter in *Cocoa Painting* (see page 28).

1. Workbox 2. Tape cutter 3. Modelling tools 4. Ball tool 5. Ribbon inserter 6. Auger tool 7. Fuse wire 8. Tullen scissors 9. Tube cleaning brush 10. Tweezers 11. Scissors 12. Florist wire 13. Crimpers 14. Flower nails 15. Stamens 16. Egg white container 17. Wire cutters 18. Gum Arabic 19. Gum tragacanth 20. Hatpins 21. Marbles

Paper cones: These are made from greaseproof paper and are generally favoured among cake decorators for use with icing tubes. See page 18 for details on how to make paper cones.

Piping jelly: Available from specialist cake decorating shops, piping jelly (page 26) is a fun technique that can be used successfully on most types of icing. It holds its shape but does not set hard. It is piped around the edges of a design and then brushed towards the centre with a small, flat brush.

Ribbon inserter: This is a most useful tool with a flat shape about 10 mm (½ inch) wide on one end which is used to make slits in the icing to allow for the insertion of ribbon. The other end of the tool often has a point for creating a broderie anglaise effect, or a ridged cone for moulding flowers.

Roller: A small chrome or plastic roller is necessary for rolling out modelling paste for moulded flowers.

Rolling board: A wooden board with a melamine or other smooth covering is essential for rolling out modelling paste and pastillage.

Rolling pin: A good quality rolling pin is necessary for rolling out marzipan and sugarpaste. Personal preference is the deciding factor. A ribbed roller is very useful for creating various effects on clothes, plaques and so on.

Scissors: A good pair of small, sharp embroidery scissors is necessary for fine work.

Shears or wire cutters: These are used for cutting wire stems.

Smoothers: Two plastic rectangles used for smoothing the sides and top edges of the marzipan and sugarpaste on a cake.

Stamens: The centres of flowers require various stamens, some of which are shown in the relevant photographs.

Straight-edge cutter: Made from extruded acrylic with a sharp cutting edge, this was developed by my daughter to facilitate cutting ribbons or strips of pastillage or modelling paste.

Tape cutter: Used for cutting florist tape into four, making it possible to tape very fine wires smoothly and evenly.

Tube cleaning brush: This looks like a miniature bottle brush and is essential for thorough cleaning of tubes after use.

Tubes: Sometimes also referred to as nozzles, icing tubes are available under various brand names. There is no international uniformity in the way in which they are numbered by the various manufacturers, except possibly for certain of the writing tubes. It is a good idea to select the best of each brand according to your purpose. Store the tubes carefully, standing upright, to avoid damage. The most popular tubes and tubes used on the cakes in this book are illustrated on pages 20–22.

Veining and fluting tools: These tools have curved ends and are ideal for figure and flower moulding.

Workbox: Tools and equipment need to be stored neatly and safely and the box shown here is ideal.

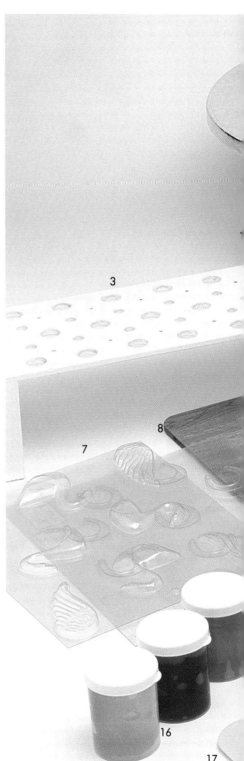

1. Turntable 2. Cake board 3. Flower stand 4. Plastic rollers 5. Ribbed roller 6. Rolling pins 7. Plastic moulds 8. Pastry board 9. Hobby knife 10. Table knives 11. Painting knife 12. Craft knife 13. Straight-edge cutters 14. Frill rulers 15. Paper cones 16. Piping jelly 17. Smoothers 18. Leaf veiners 19. Tubes 20. Orchid former

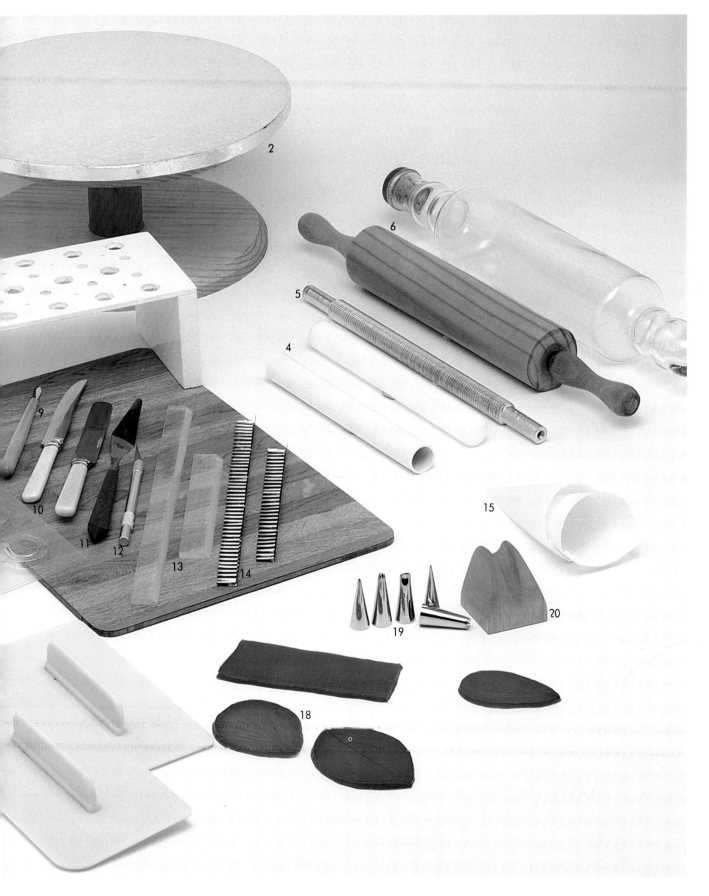

Cake and Biscuit Recipes

Over the years, I have received numerous requests for recipes which I have personally found successful. I have, therefore, included some of my favourites, together with a table of baking times and quantities for different shapes and sizes of cake tins.

Fruit Cake

750 g (1½ lb) mixed dried fruit
125 g (4 oz) dates, pitted
125 g (4 oz) glacé cherries
125 g (4 oz) nuts, chopped
125 ml (4 fl oz) brandy
250 g (8 oz) butter or margarine
250 g (8 oz) granulated sugar
6 eggs
5 ml (1 tsp) mixed spice
5 ml (1 tsp) ground cinnamon
2.5 ml (½ tsp) ground cloves
5 ml (1 tsp) ground ginger
30 ml (2 tbsp) golden syrup
375 g (12 oz) plain flour
5 ml (1 tsp) bicarbonate of soda

> *NOTE*
> *1 Should you wish to omit the dates, increase the quantity of mixed dried fruit to 875 g (1¾ lb).*
> *2 If desired, increase the quantity of mixed spice to 20 ml (4 tsp) and omit the cinnamon, cloves and ginger.*
> *3 Baked cakes are approximately 75 mm (3 inches) high.*

1 Soak the fruit and nuts overnight in brandy.

2 Preheat the oven to 150 °C (300 °F, gas mark 2).

3 Line a 225 mm (9 inch) square cake tin with greaseproof paper.

4 In a large bowl, cream the butter and sugar.

5 Add the eggs, one at a time, mixing well.

6 Add the spices and syrup.

7 Sift in the flour and continue mixing.

8 Add the fruit and nuts.

9 Mix the bicarbonate of soda with 15 ml (1 tbsp) water and add to the cake mixture. The mixture should be very thick.

10 Pour the mixture into the cake tin and bake for 2¼ hours.

11 When baked, cool the cake on a wire rack for about 30 minutes to an hour before turning out.

Fruit, Nut and Chocolate Cake

This delicious cake does not need to be iced, but makes a valuable addition to your collection of cake recipes.

250 g (8 oz) butter or margarine
250 g (8 oz) granulated sugar
4 eggs
250 g (8 oz) plain flour
60 ml (4 tbsp) milk
125 g (4 oz) mixed dried fruit
125 g (4 oz) glacé cherries, chopped
125 g (4 oz) pecan nuts, chopped
125 g (4 oz) milk chocolate, chopped
2.5 ml (½ tsp) baking powder

1 Preheat the oven to 180 °C (350 °F, gas mark 4).

2 Grease and line a 325 × 100 mm (13 × 4 inch) loaf tin.

3 Cream the butter and sugar.

4 Add the eggs one at a time, beating well after each addition.

5 Sift the flour and add to the mixture together with the milk.

6 Add the mixed dried fruit, cherries, nuts and chocolate and mix well.

7 Lastly add the baking powder.

8 Pour the mixture into the prepared tin and bake for 1½ hours.

9 Turn out on to a wire rack to cool.

Chocolate Oil Cake

Butter icing is most suitable for decorating this cake.

45 ml (3 tbsp) cocoa
100 ml (3½ fl oz) boiling water
125 g (4 oz) plain flour
good pinch salt
10 ml (2 tsp) baking powder
4 eggs
185 g (6 oz) caster sugar
60 ml (4 tbsp) oil
5 ml (1 tsp) vanilla essence
2.5 ml (½ tsp) almond essence

1 Preheat the oven to 200 °C (400 °F, gas mark 6).

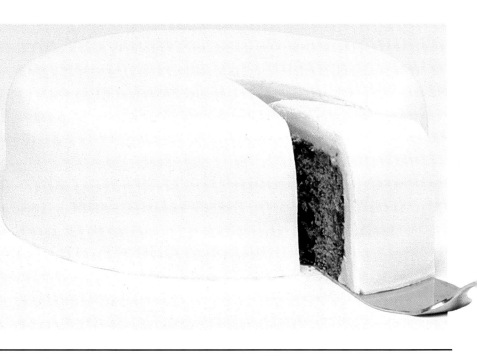

2 Grease and line two 175 mm (7 inch) sandwich tins.

3 Blend the cocoa and boiling water and allow to cool.

4 Sift together the flour, salt and baking powder.

5 Beat one egg and three yolks well, then gradually beat in the sugar and continue beating until the mixture is very thick and creamy.

6 Add the cocoa mixture, oil, vanilla and almond essence.

7 Add the flour mixture.

8 Beat the remaining egg whites until stiff peaks form and carefully fold into the cake mixture.

9 Pour the mixture into the prepared tins, tap tins gently to release the air bubbles, and bake for 25 minutes.

10 Turn out on to a wire rack to cool. When cold, fill and ice as desired.

> *NOTE: This cake freezes perfectly whether decorated or plain.*

Swiss Tea Dainties

Makes 30

125 g (4 oz) butter
90 ml (6 tbsp) caster sugar
I egg yolk
60 ml (4 tbsp) ground almonds
185 g (6 oz) plain flour
2.5 ml (½ tsp) baking powder
good pinch salt
strawberry or raspberry jam
butter or glacé icing (page 14)
glacé cherries (optional)

1 Preheat the oven to 180 °C (350 °F, gas mark 4) and grease a baking tray.

2 Cream the butter and sugar until light and fluffy.

3 Beat in the egg yolk and add the almonds.

4 Sift the flour, baking powder and salt and add to the butter mixture to form a soft dough.

5 Roll out to approximately 5 mm (¼ inch) thickness and cut into small rounds.

6 Arrange on the baking tray and bake for 10 minutes or until pale gold.

7 Cool on a wire rack and when cold, sandwich two biscuits together with raspberry or strawberry jam or butter icing.

8 Ice the top with butter or glacé icing.

9 Decorate with half a cherry if desired.

Approximate Quantities of Fruit Cake Mixture and Baking Times

The following quantities of fruit cake mixture and the baking times are approximate for the sizes and shapes of the relevant tins. It is advisable always to test each cake with a cake tester or even a knitting needle to ensure that it is sufficiently baked.

Tin size and shape	Quantity	Baking time
150 mm (6 inch) square	½ × recipe	2 hours
175 mm (7 inch) square	½ × recipe	2 hours
200 mm (8 inch) square	¾ × recipe	2 hours
225 mm (9 inch) square	1 × recipe	2¼ hours
250 mm (10 inch) square	1½ × recipe	2¾ hours
275 mm (11 inch) square	2 × recipe	3 hours
300 mm (12 inch) square	2½ × recipe	3 hours
325 mm (13 inch) square	3 × recipe	3½ hours
350 mm (14 inch) square	3½ × recipe	3½ hours
150 mm (6 inch) round	⅜ × recipe	2 hours
175 mm (7 inch) round	½ × recipe	2 hours
200 mm (8 inch) round	¾ × recipe	2 hours
225 mm (9 inch) round	¾ × recipe	2 hours
250 mm (10 inch) round	1 × recipe	2¼ hours
275 mm (11 inch) round	1½ × recipe	2¾ hours
300 mm (12 inch) round	2 × recipe	3 hours
325 mm (13 inch) round	2¼ × recipe	3½ hours
350 mm (14 inch) round	2¾ × recipe	3½ hours
400 mm (16 inch) round	4 × recipe	4½ hours
150 mm (6 inch) hexagonal★	½ × recipe	2 hours
175 mm (7 inch) hexagonal	½ × recipe	2 hours
200 mm (8 inch) hexagonal	¾ × recipe	2 hours
250 mm (10 inch) hexagonal	1½ × recipe	2¾ hours
300 mm (12 inch) hexagonal	2¼ × recipe	3½ hours
350 mm (14 inch) hexagonal	3 × recipe	3½ hours
200 mm (8 inch) petal (scalloped)	½ × recipe	2 hours
250 mm (10 inch) petal	1 × recipe	2¼ hours
300 mm (12 inch) petal	1¾ × recipe	3 hours
350 mm (14 inch) petal	2½ × recipe	3½ hours
200 × 160 mm (8 × 6½ inch) oval	½ × recipe	2 hours
250 × 200 mm (10 × 8 inch) oval	1 × recipe	2¼ hours
300 × 250 mm (12 × 10 inch) oval	1½ × recipe	2¾ hours
250 × 200 mm (10 × 8 inch) rectangle	1¼ × recipe	2¾ hours
325 × 225 mm (13 × 9 inch) rectangle	2 × recipe	3 hours
150 × 150 mm (6 × 6 inch) heart	⅜ × recipe	2 hours
225 × 200 mm (9 × 8 inch) heart	¾ × recipe	2 hours
250 × 225 mm (10 × 9 inch) heart	1 × recipe	2¼ hours
300 × 265 mm (12 × 10½ inch) heart	1½ × recipe	2¾ hours
350 × 325 mm (14 × 13 inch) heart	2 × recipe	3 hours

★ NOTE: The measurements given for hexagonal-shaped tins are from side to side.

Birthday Biscuits

Makes about 18 65 mm (2¾ inch) round biscuits. Spices or alternative flavourings may be added as desired.

150 g (5 oz) plain flour
30 g (1 oz) cornflour
2.5 ml (½ tsp) baking powder
90 g (3 oz) margarine
90 g (3 oz) caster sugar
25 ml (5 tsp) milk
few drops of vanilla essence

1 Grease a baking sheet and heat the oven to 200 °C (400 °F, gas mark 6).

2 Sift the flour, cornflour and baking powder together. Cream the margarine and caster sugar until light and fluffy. Mix in the milk, vanilla essence and flour mixture. Knead lightly.

3 Roll out to about 3 mm (⅛ in) thickness on a floured board and cut with a knife and cardboard template or with a shaped cutter.

4 Bake for about 8 minutes until golden brown. Leave the biscuits on baking sheet for 5–10 minutes before transferring to a wire rack with an egg slice.

> *NOTE: To transfer a biscuit pattern to the dough, make a template by copying the pattern on to cardboard or stiff paper and cutting it out. Place this template on rolled out dough and cut around it.*

*1. Square cake tin 2. Cup cake tins (patty pans)
3. Round cake tins 4. Cake boards 5. Biscuit cutter 6. Large, smooth-bladed knife
7. Modelling paste roller 8. Paper piping bags 9. Piping tubes 10. Biscuit templates
11. Cocktail sticks 12. Paintbrushes
13. Modelling tool 14. Craft knife*

Approximate Quantities of Beat and Mix Plain Cake

one recipe quantity = 20 to 24 cup cakes

Cake	Size	Recipe Quantity	Cake	Size	Recipe Quantity
King of Jungle *(page 34)*	200 mm (8 in) round	2	Ballerina *(page 68)*	2 × 200 mm (8 in) square	4
Alphabet *(page 48)*	300 × 225 mm (12 × 9 in)	3	Spaceship *(page 60)*	225 mm (9 in) round	1
Kitten *(page 52)*	deep 175 mm (7 in) round	1½		150 mm (6 in) bowl	⅔
	175 mm (7 in) round	½		3 large cup cakes + 3 spare	⅓
Sports Car *(page 56)*	300 mm (12 in) square	5	Happy Holidays *(page 40)*	250 mm (10 in) round	2
	150 mm (6 in) round	1			
Bo-peep *(page 36)*	175 mm (7 in) bowl	⅔	Mouse *(page 62)*	300 × 225 mm (12 × 9 in)	3
Have a Ball *(page 44)*	250 mm (10 in) square	3			

Beat and Mix Plain Cake

200 g (7 oz) plain flour
15 ml (1 tbsp) baking powder
185 g (6 oz) granulated sugar
125 g (4 oz) butter or margarine
125 ml (4 fl oz) milk
3 eggs
few drops of vanilla essence

1 Line a 200 mm (8 inch) square cake tin with greaseproof paper.

2 Preheat the oven to 160 °C (325 °F, gas mark 3).

3 Sift the dry ingredients together. Cream the butter or margarine in a bowl and add the dry ingredients, milk, eggs and vanilla essence.

4 Beat for 3 minutes at low speed with electric mixer or for 5 minutes with egg-beater, until well blended.

5 Pour the mixture into the tin and bake for 30–35 minutes or until well risen and firm to the touch.

6 Allow to cool for 5 to 10 minutes in the tin before turning out on to a wire rack.

> *NOTE: Bake cup cakes at 200 °C (400 °F, gas mark 6) for 10 minutes.*

Sandy Biscuits

Makes 56

250 g (8 oz) granulated sugar
2 eggs
3 egg yolks
300 g (10 oz) plain flour
5 ml (1 tsp) baking powder
rind of half a lemon or orange
raisins to decorate

1 Preheat the oven to 180 °C (350 °F, gas mark 4) and grease a baking tray.

2 Beat together the sugar, eggs and egg yolks until 'ribbons' form, about 3 minutes on fast speed.

3 Sift the flour and baking powder and add to the egg mixture together with lemon or orange rind, stirring gently.

4 Pipe long strips or rounds on to the baking tray.

5 Decorate with a raisin and sprinkle with granulated sugar.

6 Allow the biscuits to rest for at least 1 hour, then bake for 10–15 minutes.

Decorating Aids:

*Lollipops
Sugared almonds
Water biscuits
Ginger nut or similar biscuits, 50 mm (2 in) in diameter
Ice-cream wafer cones
Marshmallows
Spaghetti
Coloured sweets
Chocolate vermicelli*

Icing Recipes

While commercially prepared marzipan, or almond paste, and sugarpaste are available in large quantities in some areas, they may be unobtainable in country districts. I have, therefore, included the more commonly used recipes necessary to create the designs in this book.

Royal Icing

Makes about 200 g (6½ oz)

I egg white
200 g (6½ oz) icing sugar, sifted
3 drops acetic acid or 1.25 ml (¼ tsp) tartaric acid or 2.5 ml (½ tsp) lemon juice

1 Place the egg white in a clean glass bowl and beat lightly with a wooden spoon to break up the egg white.

2 Add half the icing sugar, 30 ml (2 tbsp) at a time, beating thoroughly after each addition.

3 Add the acid or lemon juice.

4 Continue adding icing sugar 30 ml (2 tbsp) at a time, until the consistency is like well-beaten cream and holds small peaks.

5 Adjust the consistency for various types of work – a firmer texture is required for piping borders, and a softer consistency for line work.

6 When colouring royal icing, use only a touch of paste colour on the end of a cocktail stick.

> NOTE: Royal icing can be mixed with an electric mixer and will take approximately 5 minutes but about 15 minutes if mixed by hand.

Fondant Icing

This icing is suitable for coating cakes and for making sweets.

Makes about 1 kg (2 lb)

250 g (8 oz) liquid glucose
I kg (2 lb) icing sugar, sifted
10 ml (2 tsp) powdered gelatine
45 ml (3 tbsp) cold water
22 g (¾ oz) white vegetable fat

1 Stand the bottle of liquid glucose, with its lid off, in hot water to warm.

2 Set aside approximately 185 g (6 oz) icing sugar.

3 Soak the gelatine in 45 ml (3 tbsp) cold water in a small container. Place the container over hot water until the gelatine has completely dissolved.

4 Melt the fat.

5 Make a well in the remaining icing sugar and add the glucose, gelatine and fat.

6 Stir well to combine. Knead the icing and adjust the consistency by either adding some of the reserved icing sugar or egg white until a smooth pliable paste is formed.

7 Store in a plastic bag in an airtight container. Do not place in the refrigerator.

Glacé Icing

This icing sets very quickly and must be used while still warm.

Makes about 155 g (5 oz)

15 ml (1 tbsp) hot water (approx)
flavouring and colouring as required
155 g (5 oz) icing sugar

1 Add water, flavouring and colouring to the icing sugar and stir until a smooth running consistency is obtained.

2 Pour over biscuits, pastry or cakes and allow to set.

> NOTE: This quantity will cover a 175 mm (7 inch) cake or 18 cup cakes.

Butter Icing

Makes about 625 g (1¼ lb)

125 g (4 oz) butter or margarine
500 g (1 lb) icing sugar
5 ml (1 tsp) flavouring
small quantity of milk, water or fruit juice

1 Cream butter very well.

2 Add icing sugar gradually.

3 Add flavouring and beat well.

4 Add a little milk, water or fruit juice until a smooth spreading consistency is formed.

Sugarpaste

Makes about 1.5 kg (3 lb)

220 g (7 oz) granulated sugar
250 g (8 oz) liquid glucose
125 ml (4 fl oz) water
10 ml (2 tsp) powdered gelatine
flavouring and colouring (optional)
I kg (2 lb) icing sugar, sifted
22 g (¾ oz) white vegetable fat

1 Place the sugar, glucose and water in a pan and heat gently to dissolve the sugar.
   Periodically wash down the sides of the saucepan with a wet pastry brush.
   Bring to the boil and place the lid on for a minute or two so that the steam can wash down the sides of the saucepan. Boil to 105 °C (220 °F) without stirring.

2 Meanwhile soak the gelatine in 15 ml (1 tbsp) cold water.

3 Remove the pan from the stove; when the bubbles subside add the gelatine. Add the flavouring and colouring and half the icing sugar.

4 Sift the remaining icing sugar on to a large wooden or other smooth surface. Make a well in the centre and pour the mixture into it. Add the vegetable fat and mix and knead until a smooth pliable consistency is obtained.

5 Roll out and coat the cake while the icing is still warm.

6 Store in a plastic bag in an airtight container. Do not place in the refrigerator.

> NOTE: This icing can be reheated in a casserole in a very cool oven.

Modelling Paste 1

This paste improves with age and should be stored in an airtight container.

Makes about 500 g (1 lb)

500 g (1 lb) sugarpaste
15 ml (1 tbsp) gum tragacanth

1 Mix the sugarpaste and gum tragacanth together and knead thoroughly. Store in a plastic bag in an airtight container. Do not store in the refrigerator.

2 Break off a piece of paste, dip it into egg white and knead it thoroughly before using.

Modelling Paste 2

Makes about 500 g (1 lb)

white margarine or vegetable fat
375 g (12 oz) icing sugar, sifted
25 ml (5 tsp) gum tragacanth (purest)
15 ml (1 tbsp) powdered gelatine
15 ml (1 tbsp) cold water
15 ml (1 tbsp) boiling water
1 large egg white

1 Grease a glass mixing bowl with white margarine or vegetable fat, add the icing sugar and place the bowl over hot water. Heat the icing sugar in the bowl.

2 Add the gum tragacanth and stir with a wooden spoon to heat evenly. Do not let the sugar become moist. Heat to just warmer than blood temperature, then remove the bowl from the water.

3 Prepare the gelatine by sprinkling it on to cold water. Add the boiling water and stand the gelatine in a bowl of hot water to dissolve. Do not place it on the cooker as gelatine must never get too hot.

4 Beat the egg white lightly with a fork to break it up.

5 Remove 250 ml (8 fl oz) warm icing sugar and keep it on one side. Add the gelatine and most of the egg white to the icing sugar in the bowl. Stir, mixing quickly. Add remaining icing sugar and beat well.

6 Transfer to a clean, greased bowl and, with clean hands greased with white margarine or vegetable fat, work the paste for 10 to 15 minutes. Add the remaining egg white if the paste seems a little dry.

7 Shape the paste into a ball, grease the outside with white margarine or vegetable fat and store it in a plastic bag in a sealed container in the refrigerator. Once or twice a week, take out the paste and work it for about 5 minutes.

Special Moulding Paste for Figures

Makes about 500 g (1 lb)

500 g (1 lb) sugarpaste
10 ml (2 tsp) gum tragacanth

1 Mix the gum tragacanth into the sugarpaste.

2 Allow to mature for at least a week before using. Store this modelling paste in a plastic bag in an airtight container. Do not store it in the refrigerator.

Marzipan 1

Makes about 1 kg (2 lb)

500 g (1 lb) ground almonds
250 g (8 oz) icing sugar
250 g (8 oz) caster sugar
10 ml (2 tsp) brandy
8 egg yolks

1 Mix all the dry ingredients together.

2 Add the brandy and sufficient egg yolk to make a paste. Do not knead too much as the marzipan will become oily. Use immediately.

Marzipan 2

Makes about 750 g (1½ lb)

500 g (1 lb) granulated sugar
250 ml (8 fl oz) water
good pinch cream of tartar
125 g (4 oz) ground almonds
1 egg, beaten
5 ml (1 tsp) ratafia or almond essence

1 Dissolve the sugar in the water over low heat. Do not allow it to boil until the sugar has completely dissolved. Wash down the sides of the saucepan with a wet pastry brush. Allow the mixture to boil to 120 °C (250 °F) without stirring.

2 Remove it from the heat and allow it to cool for exactly 20 minutes. Add cream of tartar, almonds, egg and essence and beat with a wooden spoon until thick and creamy. Leave to cool.

3 Place the marzipan on a board and knead until smooth. Use immediately.

Pastillage

Makes about 250 g (8 oz)

250 g (8 oz) royal icing
5 ml (1 tsp) gum tragacanth
dry, sifted icing sugar

1 Mix together the royal icing and gum tragacanth. Add icing sugar until you have a pliable dough that is no longer sticky.

2 Roll out on a piece of glass or board lightly dusted with cornflour and cut out the desired shapes.

3 Keep turning the shapes every few hours until evenly and thoroughly dry.

> *NOTE: Pastillage is better used at once, but can be stored in a plastic bag in an airtight container for a few hours.*

Marshmallow Paste

Makes about 155 g (5 oz)
Quantities are approximate

10 marshmallows
100 g (3½ oz) icing sugar, sifted
cornflour

1 Knead the icing sugar into the marshmallows, using your fingers, until a firm, elastic 'dough' is achieved. Colour as required.

2 Roll out with a small roller or shape as desired, using cornflour to prevent the paste from sticking to your hands.

Edible Glitter
45 ml (3 tbsp) hot water
22 g (¾ oz) gum Arabic

1 Pour water into a bowl and sprinkle gum Arabic over. Stand the bowl in hot water, stirring gently to dissolve. Strain mixture through a piece of nylon.
2 Brush mixture on to a clean baking tray and place in a warm oven until dry. Brush or scrape the dry glitter off the tray and crush it into fine flakes. Store in an airtight jar.
3 Glitter may be coloured by adding colouring to the water when mixing.

Gum Arabic Glaze
Hot water
Gum Arabic

Mix together thoroughly sufficient quantities of both to form a painting consistency. Paint on to completed moulded flowers and leaves to create a porcelain effect.

Covering a Cake

The correct preparation of a cake prior to icing is an essential part of successful cake decorating. The marzipan seals the fruit cake and prevents it from staining the icing and, together, the marzipan and icing form a smooth medium on to which you can pipe or mould your designs. A good base will make the final product look so much more professional.

3 Bring some smooth apricot jam to a full boil. Spread the hot jam very thinly over the top and sides of the cake.

4 Sprinkle dry icing sugar on to a table top or pastry board. Roll out the marzipan until it is about 5 mm (¼ inch) thick. Use the string to check that the marzipan is large enough to cover the cake comfortably. Cut off any excess.

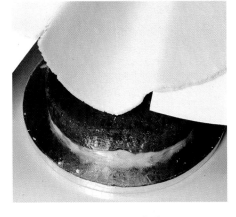

5 Slip the lifters underneath the marzipan, lift it gently and drape it over the cake. Slide out the lifters so that the marzipan falls over the cake.

6 Using a rolling pin, gently roll over the marzipan on the top of the cake and then press the marzipan against the sides of the cake with your hands.

7 Trim away the excess around the base with a knife, leaving about 3 mm (⅛ inch) around the cake. Still using your knife, press the edges of the marzipan against the base of the cake. Rub the marzipan with both hands to smooth it, taking care not to press too hard as this will leave fingermarks. Hold a set of smoothers firmly against the sides of

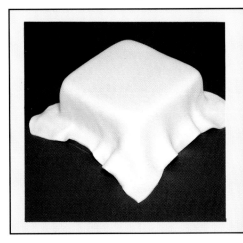

1 Place the fruit cake upside down on the cake board. (If the cake has risen to a hump or if it is uneven, trim it until it is level.) Knead the marzipan (page 15) until it is soft and pliable and place it in a plastic bag to prevent it drying out. Roll a thin 'sausage' of marzipan and fill any gaps between the cake and the board and any holes in the cake itself. Smooth over these and around the base of the cake with a knife until the whole surface is even.

2 Measure the distance over the cake with a length of string, starting at the base then up one side of the cake, across the top and down to the board on the other side. Knot the string to mark the correct length.

the cake and rub gently to further smooth the marzipan. Set the cake aside for 3 or 4 days so that the marzipan can dry out.

8 Knead and work the sugarpaste (page 14) on your pastry board, or a clean, smooth surface, until it is pliable. You may, if you wish, add 30 ml (2 tbsp) liquid glucose to each 1 kg (2 lb) of sugarpaste to keep it soft for longer. Place the sugarpaste in a plastic bag so that it does not dry out.

9 Measure the cake with a length of string, as you did for the marzipan, and tie a knot to mark the correct measurement.

10 Place the cake in a comfortable position and dampen the marzipan (either by wetting your hands and rubbing them over the marzipan, or by using a pastry-brush dipped in water), until it is evenly covered and slightly sticky – but not wet and syrupy. Wipe any water off the board.

11 Sprinkle the working surface with dry icing sugar. Place the sugarpaste on the icing sugar and roll it out, lifting it occasionally and keeping it to the shape of the cake. Do not turn the icing over. When the icing is of an even thickness, use the string to check that you have the correct size and cut away any excess. Give the icing a good 'polish' with your hands and prick any air bubbles that have emerged.

To cover a square cake
1 Lay the sugarpaste over the cake, making sure it will cover the entire cake comfortably.

2 Once the top is flat, smooth and fit the corners by cupping your hand around each corner before doing the sides.

To cover a plain cake
To cover a plain cake with sugarpaste, spread the cake with smooth apricot jam but omit the marzipan.

Assembling tiers using plastic pillars

1 Once the cake has been covered with sugarpaste, work out the position of the pillars. Make a template from paper or thin card by drawing around the cake tin. Fold the template into quarters to find the centre.

2 Mark the position of the pillars on the template by measuring the distance diagonally from the centre. Place the template on the cake and mark the positions with a pin. Remove the template.

Size of cake	Distance of pillar from centre
200 mm (8 inch)	65 mm (2½ inches)
250 mm (10 inch)	75 mm (3 inches)
300 mm (12 inch)	90 mm (3½ inches)

3 Carefully push a skewer into the cake until the point reaches the cake board. Place the pillar next to the skewer and mark the skewer level with the top of the pillar. Carefully remove the skewer and use this as a measure to cut the remaining skewers to the same length. Insert cut skewers, blunt-end first, into the cake. Place the pillars over the skewers.

Assembling tiers using extruded acrylic stands

1 Place a square or circle of paper over the stand and mark the centre of the pillars on the paper.

2 Place the paper in the centre of the covered cake and mark the positions of the pillars on the cake with a pin. Remove the paper.

3 Insert the pointed end of a skewer into the cake at each of the marked spots until the skewer touches the cake board. Remove the skewer, then re-insert it, blunt-end first, into one of the holes. With a pencil, mark the skewer level with the top of the cake, then remove the skewer and cut it at the marked spot. Cut more skewers to the same length.

4 Place a cut skewer into each of the holes in the cake. The skewers should be about 1 mm (1/16 inch) below the surface of the cake. Conceal the ends of the skewers with a little royal icing or sugarpaste. Place the extruded acrylic stand on the cake so that the pillars are positioned above each skewer.

12 Slide your hands or the lifters under the sugarpaste and lift it on to the cake, checking to see that the icing covers the entire surface of the cake.

13 Now, using your hands, gently ease the sugarpaste around the cake (if it is a square cake, start with the corners first) without making folds in the icing or tearing it. While you are working, gently rub your hands all over the cake to give a smooth, satiny finish. Trim away any excess icing at the base of the cake.

14 Use a smooth knife and firmly press the icing against the base to give a smooth, even finish.

15 Check all around the cake and smooth over any uneven patches. Use smoothers to further even the sides of the cake.

NOTE: *Approximately 1 kg (2 lb) each of sugarpaste and marzipan is required to cover a 250 mm (10 inch) cake.*

Paper Cones

If you are piping in many colours or using different tubes, make several paper cones before you start working.

Method 1

1 Use a sheet of greaseproof paper measuring approximately 680 × 420 mm (28 × 17 inches). Fold the sheet into three as shown in the diagram and with a smooth-bladed knife slit along the folds.

2 Fold each of these three pieces diagonally into two. Again slit along the fold with a knife. The sheet makes six paper cones.

3 Mark each corner of each triangular sheet as shown with A1, A2 and A3 on one side, and B1, B2 and B3 on the reverse side.

4 Hold points B2 and B1 in your left and right hands respectively. Cross corner B1 on to A2 so that A1 and A3 are facing you. Do not expect the points to be even – they should be crossing each other.

5 Holding crossed points A1 and A2 in your left hand, grasp point A3 in your right hand. Pull point A3 twice around the cone in an anti-clockwise motion.

6 Now pull point B3 sharply upwards to meet points A1 and A2 and grasp all three in your left hand.

7 With your right hand, gently pull points A2 and A3 alternately until you have a very sharp point at the tip of the cone.

8 Fold the tip of point A3 over – in towards the centre of the cone. Fold over again several times – these folds should be small folds approximately 5 mm (¼ inch) in width – until all the layers are held firmly. Smooth and press folds until the cone holds its shape firmly. All layers should be flat against one another; there should be no gaps between the layers.

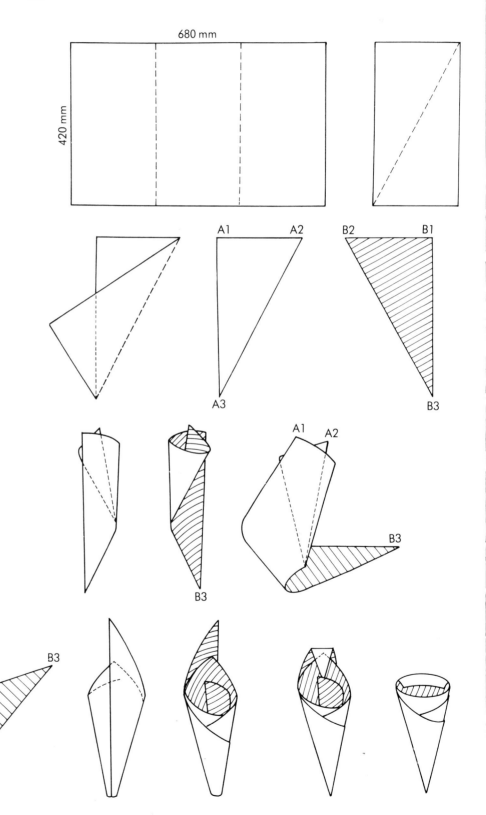

Method 2

1 Cut any size square diagonally across to make two triangles.

2 Mark the corners and one side as shown. With the long side of the triangle away from you, roll point C to meet point B and then do the same with point A.

3 Fold points A, B and C inwards, folding them several times to hold the layers firmly.

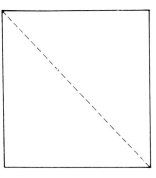

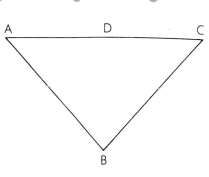

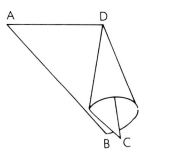 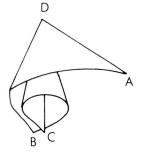 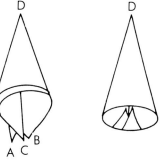 

How to fill the Paper Cone

Cut off the tip of the paper cone approximately 20 mm (¾ inch) from the point. Drop an icing tube into the cone – about half the tube should be visible. Let the cone rest in the circle made by thumb and forefinger and place a small amount of icing into the cone with a knife. Try to avoid getting any icing on the edges of the cone. Press the sides of the cone together and fold over the top edge. Then fold the corners towards the centre. Again fold the edges of the cone over a few times. A cone can be refilled and used a few times.

> NOTE: *When you are not using the filled cone, place the end of the tube into a damp cloth or sponge to prevent the icing hardening and blocking the tube. Do not, however, put the paper cone into the wet cloth.*

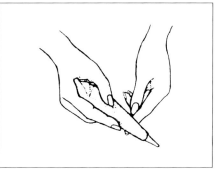

How to hold an Icing Cone

The best way to hold an icing cone (or bag) is in such a way that you can press with your thumb while holding the cone, almost as you would hold a pen or pencil. Learn to press with one hand only, although you may guide with the other.

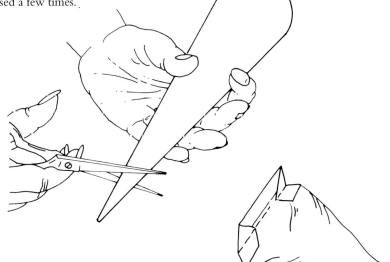

Icing Tubes

Tubes, and equivalents, used in this book:

Brand	Star Tubes	Writing Tubes	Ribbon Tubes
Ateco	16, 18, 33	1, 2, 4	98, 47
Bekenal	6, 7, 8, 37	1, 2, 3	22
Probus	6, 7, 8, 13	1, 2, 3	12, 9, 34
Tala	6, 7, 8, 13	1, 2, 3	12, 34

Decorating Techniques

Tubework or piping is an essential part of cake decorating. With practice, you will soon master the fine art of decorating a cake using royal icing and a tube. The following pages will take you through the various basic techniques such as lines, loops, shells, scrolls, embroidery, lace pieces, basket weave and so on. In addition, full colour, step-by-step photographs illustrate simply and clearly the techniques of piping flowers as these are an integral part of this decorative art form.

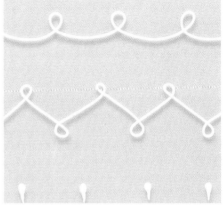

Exercises on Glass

It is very useful to practise on a sheet of glass as it is easy to keep clean and enables you to make certain of mastering a step or technique before working on an actual cake. Later on, when you begin to learn more difficult designs, a pattern can be placed under the glass which you can follow while working on top.

ICING TUBES

Writing tubes: These are used for writing messages on cakes, making dots, lines, loops, embroidery, snail's trails, and also for figure piping (page 25). Generally, these tubes are the lower numbers in the range, for example 00, 0, 1, 2, and so on.

A very useful exercise for piping *lines* and *loops* is to touch the work surface with the end of the tube, press on the cone and then lift the tube about 35–40 mm (1½–1¾ inches) away from the glass or cake, pressing constantly and not stretching the icing, so that the icing falls into place on the surface.

When forming *dots* and *beads*, it is difficult to disguise the tail. For small dots, the icing should be soft. Use very little pressure on the cone; just enough to make a tiny dot. For larger dots use constant pressure and keep the point of the tube stationary in the bead or dot until it is the size required. Release pressure and move the cone gently in a circle before removing the tube. Gently press any projecting point down into the dot or bead, if necessary.

Cornelli or scribbling is done with No. 00, 0 or 1 writing tubes using a maze of Ws and Ms in a continuous line but at random. You should not be able to see where the work begins or ends.

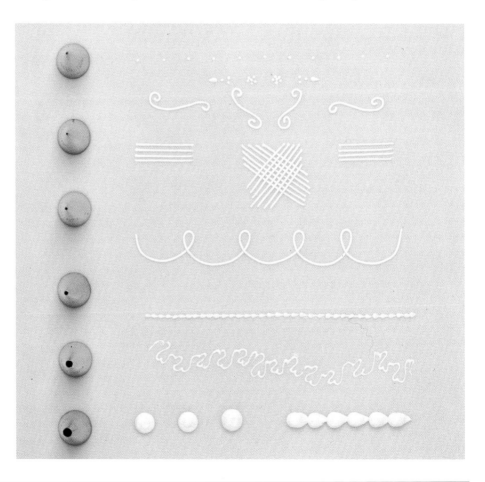

Star tubes: There is a very large range of star tubes available. These are used for making shells, stars, scrolls and so on. Make sure the icing is the correct consistency – it should form a firm peak when a knife is lifted out of the icing.

To create *stars*, hold the cone, fitted with the appropriate tube, perpendicular to the surface. Press the cone firmly to release the icing, stop pressing, then remove the cone.

To form *shells*, use any of the star tubes available and hold the icing cone at a 45 ° angle. With the tip of the tube touching the surface of the work, press very firmly. Move the tube slightly away from the surface giving the icing room to build up. Ease off pressing, then stop pressing, tapering off the icing by pulling the cone towards you. You have now formed the first shell. Now, just touching on the end of the first, start the next shell, ensuring that the untidy start of the icing does not show and again, pressing very firmly, repeat the procedure.

To create *pull-up shells* around the side of a cake, repeat the same procedure in an upwards direction.

Rosettes are piped with a deep-cut star tube, that is either a Probus No. 13 or Ateco No. 33, moved in a circular motion.

Petal tubes: These can be either straight, such as Probus No. 42 or Ateco No. 101, or curved, such as the Bekenal No. 57, and are used for any royal icing flowers such as roses, daisies, and so on. An exception is the horseshoe shape, Ateco No. 81, used for chrysanthemums and lily-of-the-valley.

Drop flower tubes, which make a whole flower with one pressing of the icing cone, are also available in many varieties, for example Probus No. 31 and Ateco No. 224. My favourite is the Bekenal No. 37 drop flower tube as it is very easy to use and is most effective on children's birthday cakes.

Special effect tubes: For a shell and ruffle border, the Ateco Nos. 86, 87 and 88 are very effective. The grass or hair tube, Ateco No. 233, is very useful on children's birthday cakes. Multiple hole tubes can be used most successfully in various ways, for example there is one with five holes in a row which can be used for writing lines of music on a cake.

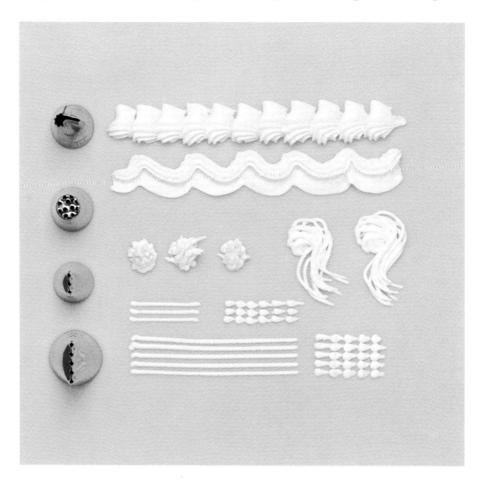

Ribbon tubes: One or both edges are serrated and these can be used for piping ribbons or bands and also for basket weave, for example Bekenal No. 22. Included here is the curved tube, Ateco No. 98 (sometimes referred to as a shell tube) which is the one I like to use for basket weave (page 24).

Leaf tubes: While one can use a paper cone to pipe leaves, there are very good leaf tubes available in three sizes, namely the Ateco Nos. 349, 350 and 352.

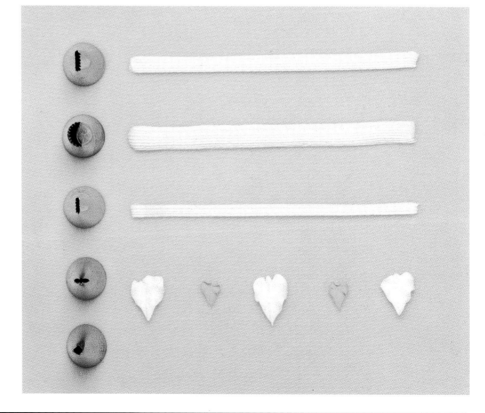

FLOODWORK

Floodwork, or run-in-work, is the art of filling in a picture with royal icing thinned to the right consistency. It is advisable to do more than one picture at a time so that, while one section is drying, you can work on a section in another picture. Floodwork items will keep very well in a strong box protected from dust and bumps.

Mix royal icing to a firm peak consistency and then thin down half of it with a few drops of water. Use an eye dropper to get the consistency exactly right. Do not beat the icing when adding the water but stir it gently. It is preferable to allow the icing to stand for 12 hours so that any bubbles can subside.

When a knife is drawn through it, the thinned icing should only come together after a slow count of ten. Icing which is too thin does not set well.

It is important to dry floodwork quickly to retain its shine. If you are working on a rainy day, use a heater or the warming drawer to dry the floodwork.

1 Place the picture to be flooded under glass and stick it in place at the corners with a little royal icing. Tape a piece of waxed (not greaseproof) paper to the glass, ensuring that there is at least a 25 mm (1 inch) margin around the edge of the picture. Do make sure that there are no wrinkles in the paper. If the design has a middle opening (like a collar, for example) you may cut a small cross in the centre of the paper to relax the natural tension of the paper. Any buckling or wrinkling of the paper may cause the design to break.

2 Outline the picture using firm peak royal icing in a small writing tube.

3 Fill a paper cone with thinned icing, but do not cut the hole in the bottom until you are ready to fill in the design otherwise the icing will flow out. It is not necessary to use a tube. Make sure the hole is not too big, or the icing may flow out too quickly, overrunning your lines. Start close to your outline, but do not touch it with the cone as it may break. Always start filling in the part of the picture that is furthest away from you. For example, of two trees one behind the other, you would do the back one first.

Keep the tip of the bag close to the surface to reduce the formation of air bubbles and let the icing flow out, moving the bag backwards and forwards across the shape.

4 When flooding a collar for a cake, flood a section and then flood alternately on either side of that section. This prevents the icing from setting and leaving a line.

5 When the area is almost filled, use a small paintbrush to push the icing to the outline to form a smooth edge. If any bubbles appear, immediately smooth them away with a paintbrush or hatpin.

6 Once the floodwork is dry, slide the piece of paper with the floodwork on to the edge of the table. Gently pull the paper downwards against the edge of the table while supporting the floodwork with your other hand. Keep turning the picture so that the paper is removed evenly all round. Do not extend the floodwork more than 50 per cent beyond the table edge.

7 To attach a collar, pipe a line of icing with a No. 2 writing tube all around the top edge of the cake and then position the collar on this line. When positioning smaller pieces on a cake, it is easier to paint the back of the floodwork piece with royal icing before attaching it.

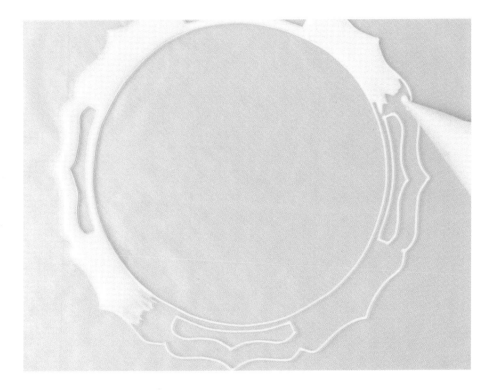

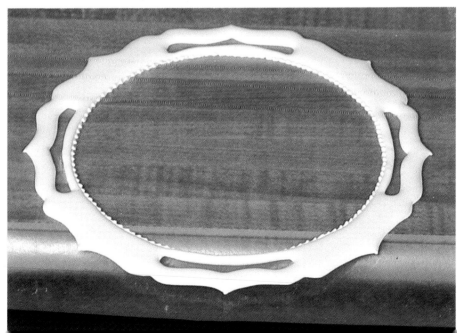

GLASS STENCILS

I have found this technique invaluable for transferring embroidery designs, lettering or pictures on to a cake.

1 Trace the design on to a piece of paper. Carefully outline the design on the back of the paper with a pencil.

2 Place the design under the glass so that the pencilled outlines are facing you. Fill a paper cone with royal icing and, using a small writing tube, pipe directly on to the glass (the lettering or design will be back-to-front). Allow the icing to dry.

3 When the icing is quite hard, press the design against fresh sugarpaste. Lift the glass away and you will have the design on your cake exactly where you want it.

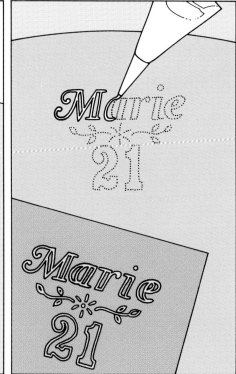

ROPING

1 Fill a cone with royal icing and use a small or medium star tube, or a large writing tube, to create a twisted rope. Hold the cone at a 45 ° angle and pipe a 'comma' curving downwards, then to the left, flicking slightly to the right as you end off. Keep constant pressure on the cone as you work.

BASKET WEAVE

Weaving is achieved by using a ribbon tube (where one edge is serrated and the other straight) and royal icing.

1 Pipe a vertical line the required length on to the work surface, then do a number of short lines across the first vertical line, leaving a space the width of your tube between them.

2 Now do another vertical line, just covering the ends of the short ones.

3 Pipe short lines over this vertical line so that the start of your short line looks as though it is coming from underneath the first long vertical line. Continue in this way, filling in all the spaces along the last vertical line. Repeat this procedure until you have covered the area required.

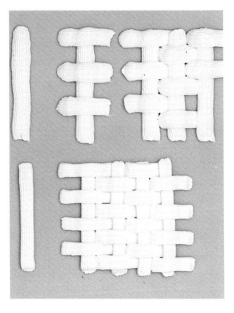

FIGURE PIPING

Figure piping may be executed with any size writing tube but, of course, the size of the tube will determine the size of the figure. Use royal icing that is firm enough to hold its shape when piped into a ball but not so stiff as to form ridges. No patterns are required as figure piping is done freehand. Use constant pressure and keep the end of the tube in the icing while piping.

Tiny teddy bear: Use a No. 0 writing tube and royal icing and pipe the body, head, arms, legs and ears, in that order, on to a piece of waxed paper. When the teddy is dry, remove it and attach it to the cake with royal icing.

Bunny: Using white royal icing in a No. 2 writing tube, pipe the bunny as shown on to waxed paper and allow it to dry. Remove the bunny and attach it to the cake with royal icing.

Baby face: Pipe the face on to waxed paper with soft flesh-coloured royal icing in a No. 3 or 4 writing tube and allow it to dry

thoroughly. Paint the eyes and mouth with food colouring. With white royal icing in a No. 3 or 4 writing tube, pipe a large ball on to waxed paper to form the bonnet. Immediately attach the face by pushing it into this ball. If desired, trim the bonnet with tiny royal icing dots using a No. 0 or 1 writing tube and leave it to dry thoroughly.

RIBBON BOWS

Ribbon bows made from florist ribbon are very useful decorations for celebration cakes. They are usually made from strips of ribbon about half a metre/yard long and of any width. Make a few bows in different sizes and colours and keep them ready for use.

1 Cut a length of ribbon 500 mm (20 inches) long and 10 mm (½ inch) wide. At one end make a loop about 25 mm (1 inch) long so that the end hangs below the short one.

2 Fold the long end so that the right side is uppermost, then make another loop to form the other half of the bow.

3 Fold underneath again so that the right side is uppermost and continue until no more loops can be made.

4 Cut a length of wire about 50 mm (2 inches) long and bend it over the centre of the ribbon to hold the latter firmly together, then twist the wire tightly.

5 Pull the loops so that they all point in the same direction.

6 Curl the loose end of the bow using the blade of a pair of scissors. Attach the bow to the cake with royal icing, by inserting it into a small mound of sugarpaste or by taping it to flower sprays.

PIPING JELLY

Piping jelly is a most effective medium on cakes and can be used most successfully on butter icing, royal icing, rice paper, sugarpaste and on its own. Piping jelly is available in red, green, yellow, neutral and clear, although other colours can be created successfully with the addition of food colouring. It is used in a paper cone with a sharp point or, alternatively, in a cone with a tube.

To show the versatility of this medium, the designs have all been executed on cake boards covered with sugarpaste.

1 Pipe the design on to a piece of glass or extruded acrylic with royal icing and a No. 0 writing tube. Allow to dry. Cover the cake board with sugarpaste and immediately press the glass stencil into the icing.

2 Colour some piping jelly with food colouring (or with coloured royal icing in equal parts of piping jelly and icing). Put the piping jelly into a small paper cone without a tube and cut off the tip to make a hole the size of a No. 2 writing tube.

3 Have a small paintbrush handy (preferably a flat one 3–5 mm (⅛–¼ inch) wide).

4 Pipe the jelly all around the edge of the design and then brush the edge of the piping jelly towards the centre, leaving a raised edge. Pipe in berries or dots as required.

5 Pipe shells or stars around the edges of the cake board using royal icing in a star tube.

COCOA PAINTING

Cocoa painting is a technique which gives effective and impressive results yet is very simple to execute. The secret of cocoa painting is to create a contrast between light and shade.

Work on a pastillage plaque or directly on to the sugarpaste on a cake, using the appropriate brush size to fit the picture.

1 Trace your chosen picture on to a piece of tracing paper. Using a soft pencil, go over the design on the back of the paper.

2 Place the picture on the plaque or cake and gently rub or trace over the lines with a sharp object to transfer the tracing on to the icing.

3 Place three small quantities of cocoa butter, each approximately the size of a large pea, into three hollows of a plastic artist's palette, or use an egg poacher.

4 To the first one add about 5 ml (1 tsp) cocoa powder. To the next, add a little less cocoa and to the third one even less.

5 Place the artist's palette over a bowl of boiling water and mix the cocoa and cocoa butter together with a cocktail stick. You will now have three shades of cocoa for painting.

6 Start with the lightest or the medium shade and outline the main features or areas.

7 Gradually deepen the shading on the picture, completing it by using the darkest shade of cocoa to contrast the lighter or 'white' areas.

8 Should the cocoa butter mixture harden making it difficult to paint, re-heat it over a bowl of boiling water.

Floral Decorations

Rose and Bud

Equipment
florist wire
florist tape
pale pink, pale and dark green modelling paste
(page 15)
patterns for calyx and rose petals (page 72)
egg white
ball tool
small scissors

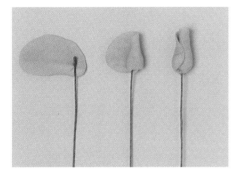

1 Cut green florist tape into four, cover a piece of florist wire and bend over one end. Roll pale pink modelling paste, the size of a large pea, into a ball. Roll into a 'sausage' and then flatten along the length of this roll, flattening one side only.

2 Dip the curved end of the covered florist wire into egg white and place it into one end of the modelling paste. Roll the modelling paste against itself to make a centre for the rose. Set aside to dry.

3 Add the calyx at this stage to form a rosebud. *If a half rose is desired, continue from Step 9 for instructions on how to mould the petals.* Colour modelling paste green and

add a touch of brown. Now take a small portion of this paste and add white to it to form a very pale green. Roll out each shade separately, then place one on top of the other, attaching the two layers with egg white if necessary.

4 Roll out the two layers together and cut out the calyx using a calyx cutter or a calyx pattern. Lift the calyx with a flat knife and place it, dark side up, on the palm of your hand.

5 Move the small end of a ball tool along the length of each sepal and then hollow out the centre of the calyx. Pinch the ends of each sepal to make a point. With small scissors cut a tiny strip away from the base of each sepal.

6 Turn the calyx over and paint egg white on its centre and a little way along each sepal.

7 Join the calyx to the rose by pushing the wire stem through the centre of the calyx. The light side goes against the rose.

8 Roll a piece of darker green paste into a ball the size of a small pea. Flatten one side slightly, paint the flattened side with egg white and push the wire stem through the ball, flat side uppermost, to form the hip of the rose.

9 Roll out pink modelling paste and cut out three smaller rose petals with a petal

cutter or use a pattern and a sharp knife. Place a petal in the palm of your hand; hollow and flute it with a ball tool.

10 Paint the base of each petal with egg white and attach each to the cone, curving the edges outward. Set aside to dry. Following Steps 3–8 above, add the calyx at this stage to form a half rose.

11 For a fuller rose, cut out five larger petals and hollow and flute the petals with a ball tool in the palm of your hand. Paint with egg white and attach to the cone with the three petals attached. Add the calyx, following Steps 3–8 above, and gently curve back the sepals of the calyx.

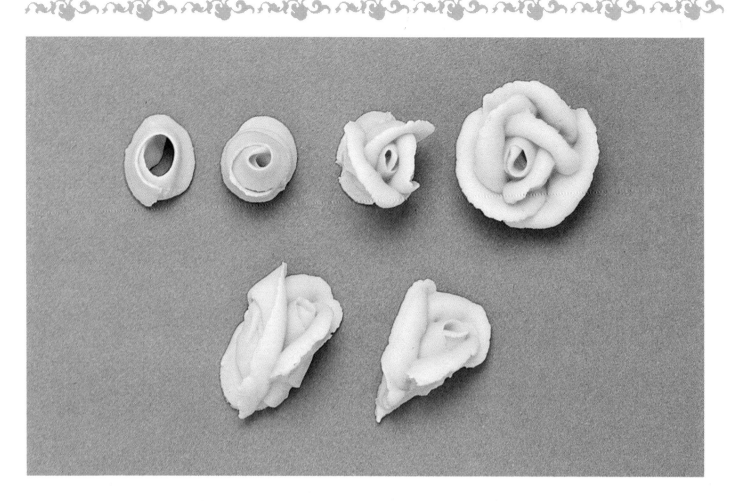

Rose Flower and Bud

Equipment
40 mm (1¾ inch) square waxed paper
flower nail
large petal tube
250 g (8 oz) pale pink royal icing (page 14)

1 Attach the waxed paper to the flower nail with a dot of royal icing. Fill a large petal tube and a paper cone with pale pink icing.

2 Hold the tube against the waxed paper on the flower nail and at right angles to it. With the wide end of the tube to the centre of the nail, press the cone, and when the icing comes through, pull the cone towards you as though you are pulling down a lever. When the side of the tube is touching the nail, turn the nail in your left hand (right hand if left-handed) in a clockwise direction (anti-clockwise if left-handed) allowing the icing to wrap around the icing already on the nail, thus forming a cone.

3 End off by turning the nail but holding the tube steady in the one position until you have completely circled the cone. Stop pressing and turn the nail and pull the tube away in the same direction ending low on the cone and close to the nail.

4 Continue building this cone of icing by wrapping another 'band' of icing around the icing on the nail. Hold the paper cone at a 45 ° angle with the tube close to the top of the icing on the nail and almost touching it. This cone will form the centre of the rose. Repeat this process once more so that the cone is 15 mm (¾ inch) high.

5 Touch the wide end of the tube to the flower cone about halfway up, with the narrow part of the tube towards your left and away from the icing. Press and turn your right hand from the wrist to the right in an 'up and over' movement, rather like opening a fan. Pipe two more in this way.

6 Hold the tube in the same position as for the first three petals, but start at the base of the cone, in line with the centre of the first petal, right against the nail. Move up and over, turning your hand from the wrist from left to right and finish the petal in line with the centre of the next petal of the previous row. Pipe two more petals in the same way.

7 You have now completed the rose. Carefully remove the waxed paper and rose from the nail and set it aside to dry thoroughly.

Rosebud

1 Proceed as for the rose flower, but after the first three petals shake the nail gently so that the cone falls on to its side and the 'V' formed by two of the petals is facing you.

2 Use a hatpin to cut away the excess icing on either side of the base of the bud.

NOTE: The rose can be piped directly on to a cocktail stick instead of on to a flower nail. Touch the end of the cocktail stick in some white margarine or vegetable fat and then pipe the rose directly on to it. Remove gently when the flower has set.

Carnation

Equipment
modelling paste (page 15)
pattern (page 72)
icing knife, hobby knife or small scissors
auger tool
water
covered florist wire
green florist tape
paintbrush
food colourings
white stamens

1 To make a small flower, roll out the modelling paste thinly and, using the pattern, cut out a scalloped round about 50 mm (2 inches) in diameter. Using an icing knife, cut tiny slits in the paste all round the edge.

2 Frill the edge of the circle with an auger tool. Paint a cross on the modelling paste with water and pinch the centre of the circle from underneath to form a point, making sure that the edges do not stick to one another. Open up the flower with the auger tool to give it a 'fluffy' appearance.

3 Push the looped end of a piece of covered florist wire through the flower and allow it to dry. When dry, you may tape a piece of green florist tape around the base.

4 To make a large flower, repeat Steps 1 and 2 above three or four times and then join the parts with water, pressing them together to form a large carnation. (Touch the edges of the petals with a paintbrush dipped in red or pink food colouring, if desired.)

5 Roll a ball of green modelling paste about half the size of a marble and hollow out the centre into a cup shape. Thin the edge with your fingers and then cut it into five equal sections. Cut each section into a pointed shape.

6 Thread a piece of covered florist wire, with a closed hook at one end, through the calyx and then stick a small ball of green paste on top of the wire inside the calyx to secure it. Paint the inside of the calyx with water. Attach the calyx to the flower by inserting the flower into the hollowed calyx.

7 Cut three lengths of white stamen 'stalk' and curl one end of each by scraping the blade of a pair of scissors or the back of a knife along it. Dip the straight ends of the stamens into water and then insert them into the centre of the carnation.

Long-stemmed Carnation

To make a long-stemmed carnation, tape an extra length of wire to the stem. Cut pieces of florist tape into leaf shapes and twist them on to the stem where required.

Putting on the Ritz

A stunning design with a masculine bias – the moulded accessories are shown to advantage on the smooth white surface.

Ingredients
1 × 250 mm (10 inch) octagonal cake
1 kg (2 lb) white sugarpaste (page 14)
black and white modelling paste (page 15)
white and black royal icing (page 14)

Materials and Decorations
1 × 300 mm (12 inch) octagonal cake board
5 mm (¼ inch) wide black ribbon
pattern for gloves (page 75)
1 long-stemmed red carnation (page 31)
tubes: Nos. 1 and 3

NOTE: *The quantity of fruit cake mixture required for an octagonal cake of this size is approximately the same as for a 250 mm (10 inch) round cake.*

1 Cover the cake with white sugarpaste.

2 Make the top hat by rolling a black modelling paste cylinder, about 50 mm (2 inches) high and 50 mm (2 inches) in diameter.

3 Roll out some black modelling paste to a thickness of about 2.5 mm (⅛ inch) and cut out a 75 mm (3 inch) diameter circle to form the brim of the hat. Allow to dry.

4 Moisten the base of the cylinder and attach it to the brim. Complete the hat adding a band of black ribbon.

5 Mould the cane in black modelling paste to fit across the top of the cake. Add a knob of white modelling paste to the top of the cane and allow to dry.

6 Roll out some white modelling paste to a thickness of about 2.5 mm (⅛ inch) and cut out the gloves, using the pattern.

7 Mark three lines into the tops of the gloves to resemble stitching.

8 Position the items on the cake, attaching them with royal icing.

9 Add an appropriate message or name.

10 Using a No. 3 tube and white royal icing, pipe large beads (page 20) around the top and base of the cake.

11 Pipe scallops (page 20) around the white beads with a No. 1 tube and black royal icing.

12 Finally, pipe dots around the scallops on the board, using a No. 1 tube and black royal icing.

King of the Jungle

Prepare a roaring party feast with this lion's face cake, elephant and giraffe biscuits and chewy crocodile novelties.

The Cake

Ingredients
1 × 200 mm (8 inch) diameter round cake
40 mm (1¾ inches) deep
2 ginger nut biscuits (or similar biscuits,
50 mm (2 inches) in diameter)
750 g (1½ lb) golden yellow butter icing
brown and white butter icing (page 14)
2 cup cakes

Materials and Decorations
275 mm (11 inch) round cake board
6 paper piping bags
tubes: No. 4 writing and No. 18 star

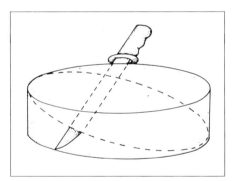

1 Cut cake diagonally as shown, to form two equal halves.

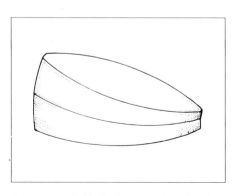

2 Turn top half of cake around so that the two thicker edges lie together.

3 Soften 100 g (3½ oz) yellow butter icing and spread over top of cake. Smooth with a knife dipped in boiling water.

4 Position cup cakes on face to form muzzle and attach with butter icing.

5 Attach ginger nut biscuits to head to form ears, packing a little butter icing beneath them to raise them slightly.

6 Mark eyebrows and outline of eyes using a cocktail stick, then pipe in with brown icing and No. 4 tube.

7 Using white icing and No. 18 tube, pipe stars (page 20) on cup cake muzzle. Pipe dots and mouth with brown icing and No. 4 tube.

8 Place some brown icing in a piping bag and cut off tip 5 mm (¼ inch) from point. Pipe a large dot for nose.

9 Soften white butter icing to flooding consistency with water. Using piping bag with tip cut off, pipe centre of ears and whites of eyes. Soften brown butter icing and pipe centres of eyes.

10 Cut 10 mm (½ inch) off tip of piping bag filled with softened, golden yellow butter icing and pipe a circle around edge of each ear. Smooth icing with knife if necessary.

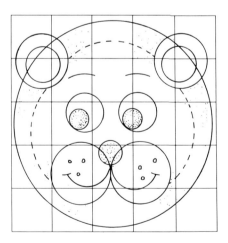

11 Use golden yellow butter icing and No. 18 tube to pipe lion's mane (add more colouring to vary shade of mane, if desired). Start piping mane around base of cake where it rests on board: touch tube to cake, squeeze piping bag firmly so that icing

adheres to cake, then pull tube away from cake to leave a tapering yellow strand.

12 Continue to pipe yellow strands around lion's head until entire side of cake is covered. Pipe final strands on surface of cake, up to dotted line marked on pattern.

Crocodile

Ingredients
250 g (8 oz) green marshmallow paste (page 14)
white and black royal icing
cornflour

Materials and Decorations
craft knife or small, sharp scissors
2 small paper piping bags

1 Roll 25 mm (1 inch) diameter ball of modelling paste into a 75 mm (3 inch) long sausage which tapers at either end. Use cornflour to prevent paste from sticking to hands.

2 Pinch top of sausage to form crocodile's

back and a ridge along its tail. Pinch a ridge on the head then divide it to form eyes.

3 Roll four small sausages to make legs. Flatten one end of each sausage and cut to form toes. Dampen other end and attach legs to body.

4 Use knife or scissors to slit snout horizontally, forming mouth. Make small slits on tail.

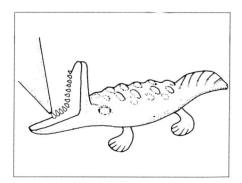

5 Open mouth wide and pipe teeth, using

white royal icing in a piping bag with tip cut off. Close mouth to desired position.

6 Pipe a black royal icing dot on top of a white dot to make eyes. Pinch end of snout and make two small hollows for nostrils. Curve tail slightly. Leave to dry.

Animal Biscuits

Ingredients
10 biscuits, cut and baked in animal shapes (use biscuit cutters or make templates)
brown, yellow and pale blue royal icing

Materials and Decorations
3 paper piping bags
tube: No. 2 writing

1 Pipe outline on each biscuit, using appropriate colour.

2 Flood each biscuit using thinned royal icing. Pipe on other details.

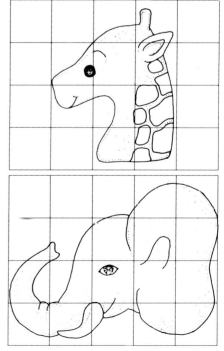

Little Bo-Peep

Bring a nursery rhyme to life for the birthday child with this lovely stand-up cake and the fluffy marshmallow sheep.

The Cake

Ingredients
1 × 175 mm (7 inch) diameter (at widest surface) dome-shaped cake, baked in oven-proof bowl, 150 mm (6 inches) deep
white sugarpaste (page 14)
pink, brown and white butter icing
brown modelling paste (page 15)
yellow, white and pink royal icing (page 14)

Materials and Decorations
250 mm (10 inch) round cake board
doll, 225 mm (9 inches) tall
6 paper piping bags
tubes: No. 2 writing, No. 16 and 18 star and No. 33 star

1 Place cake, top surface down, on board. Knead sugarpaste until pliable.

2 Remove doll's legs and place doll on top of cake. Secure doll with sugarpaste, smoothing icing up to her waist to form top of skirt.

3 Soften 45 g (1½ oz) pink butter icing with a little boiling water and spread over cake. Smooth icing with a knife dipped in boiling water.

4 With pink butter icing and a No. 16 tube pipe stars (page 20) on to doll to form bodice and sleeves of dress.

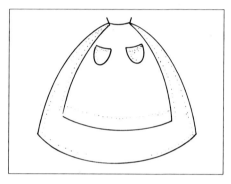

5 Using brown butter icing and a No. 2 tube pipe outline of apron and pockets on skirt.

6 Pipe white butter icing stars using a No. 16 tube, around base of cake to form frill, and within outlines of apron and pockets.

7 With pink icing in a No. 18 tube, pipe stars over rest of skirt.

8 With brown icing and a No. 2 tube pipe dots around edges of sleeves and on apron, 10 mm (½ inch) from bottom edge. Pipe buttons.

9 Make a crook by rolling a 200 mm (8 inch) long sausage of brown modelling paste and curving it into a crook shape. When dry, tie a ribbon around top and fix crook in position on cake, using butter icing.

10 Attach pink piped flowers where desired.

Marshmallow Sheep

Ingredients
10 white marshmallows
white and black butter icing (page 14)

Materials and Decorations
scissors
40 × 35 mm (1½ inch) lengths of wooden skewer or lollipop stick
2 paper piping bags
tubes: No. 2 writing and No. 16 star

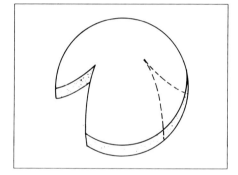

1 To make sheep's head, dip scissors in boiling water and cut 5 mm (¼ inch) slice off each marshmallow. Make two V-shaped cuts on either side of slice to form ears and chin. Keep one cut-out section for tail.

2 Push four 35 mm (1½ inch) sticks into marshmallow body to form legs. Twist sticks backwards and forwards as you push them in to ensure that they are firmly inserted.

3 Pipe stars (page 21) over entire body using white butter icing and a No. 16 tube.

4 Attach head and tail to body with icing and pipe eyes and mouth with black icing and a No. 2 tube.

Strawberry Celebration

This colourful birthday cake with a fruity theme can be adapted to suit any occasion.

Ingredients
1 × 250 mm (10 inch) octagonal cake
1.5 kg (3 lb) white sugarpaste (page 14)
yellow royal icing (page 14)
red, green and white modelling paste (page 15)

Materials and Decorations
1 × 300 mm (12 inch) octagonal cake board
pattern for lettering (pages 78–79),
leaves (page 72)
tracing paper
tube: No. 1
non-toxic gold powder
little gin, vodka or caramel oil flavouring
cocktail stick
florist wire
small star-shaped cutter
egg white
5-petal flower cutter
yellow stamens
pin

1 Cover the cake and the board with white sugarpaste.

2 If liked, using the lettering on pages 78–79, trace 'Happy Birthday' on to a piece of tracing paper and transfer it to the top of the cake by going over the letters with a sharp object. Outline the letters with yellow royal icing in a No. 1 writing tube and then flood them with yellow royal icing, following the instructions for Floodwork on page 23. Mix the gold powder with a little gin, vodka or caramel oil flavouring and paint the letters once they have dried.

3 Mould red modelling paste into strawberries of different sizes, including some tiny 'young' ones with the calyx still wrapped around the fruit.

4 Prick tiny holes all over the strawberries with a cocktail stick. Pipe a dot of yellow royal icing into each hole using a No. 1 writing tube. Smooth off each dot with your fingers. Insert a piece of florist wire into each strawberry and bud.

5 Using the star-shaped cutter, cut small stars out of green modelling paste for the hulls and attach them to the strawberries with egg white.

6 Roll out white modelling paste and cut out the flowers using the 5-petal flower cutter. Hollow them slightly and thread a piece of florist wire that has been bent at one end through the centre of each flower.

7 Pipe yellow royal icing into each flower to form the centre and insert a few small, yellow stamens into the icing while it is still wet. Allow to dry thoroughly.

8 Roll out green modelling paste and cut out leaves using the pattern on page 72. Vein the leaves with a pin as shown.

9 Attach the strawberries, leaves and flowers to the cake with royal icing.

Happy Holidays

Brighten up a summer birthday party with this smiling, sunny cake. Ice-cream wafer cones and crunchy beach balls and sundaes add a festive touch.

The Cake

Ingredients
1 × 250 mm (10 inch) round cake,
50 mm (2 inches) deep
brown, yellow and orange butter icing (page 14)
chocolate vermicelli

Materials and Decorations
300 mm (12 inch) round cake board
cocktail sticks
waxed paper
3 paper piping bags
tubes: No. 4 writing and No. 18 star

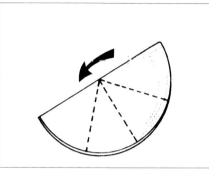

1 Cut a 250 mm (10 inch) diameter circle out of paper. Fold circle in half. Fold paper in half two more times. Lay out flat – you should have eight divisions.

2 Copy the pattern of sun face on to paper (inner circle has a diameter of 150 mm (6 inches) and cut out. Attach pattern to cake with cocktail sticks.

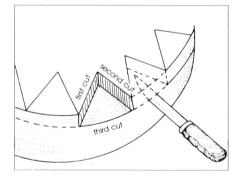

3 Cut rays of sun, holding knife vertically and taking care not to cut deeper than 20 mm (¾ inch) below cake surface. Hold knife horizontally and undercut the triangles between rays. Remove triangles of cake, and pattern.

4 Pour chocolate vermicelli on to waxed paper. Soften 125 g (4 oz) brown butter icing with boiling water and spread thinly over sides of cake. Gently roll cake over vermicelli to coat iced sides.

5 Soften 75 g (2½ oz) yellow butter icing and spread on vertical sides of rays of sun and over centre circle.

6 Using brown butter icing and a No. 4 tube pipe around centre circle of cake. Mark eyes, eyebrows, nose, mouth and cheeks with a cocktail stick.

7 Pipe stars (page 20) on top surface of rays of sun and on cheeks, using orange butter icing and a No. 18 tube.

8 Pipe eyes, eyebrows, nose and mouth using brown butter icing and a No. 4 tube.

9 Use yellow butter icing and a No. 18 tube to pipe stars on face and on triangular surfaces between rays of sun.

Beach Balls and Sunny Sundaes

Ingredients
10 birthday biscuits, cut and baked in 65 mm (2¾ inch) diameter circles for beach balls
10 biscuits, cut and baked in sundae shapes
red, green, yellow, pink and brown royal icing (page 14)
white butter icing (page 14)

Materials and Decorations
5–6 paper piping bags
tube: No. 2 writing
3 drinking straws, each cut into 4 pieces

1 Outline and flood biscuits.

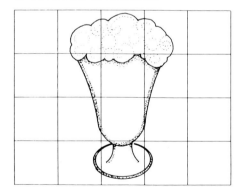

2 When flooded sundaes have set, place butter icing in paper piping bag and cut 5 mm (¼ inch) off tip. Pipe frothy top on to sundaes using a circular motion. Insert piece of drinking straw into butter icing.

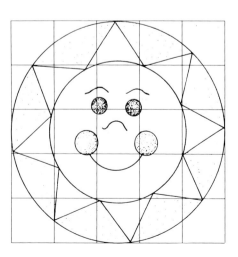

Ice-Cream Cone Biscuits

Ingredients
5 wafer biscuits
8 marshmallows
white or pink butter icing (page 14)

Materials and Decorations
scissors
1 small paper piping bag

1 Cut wafer biscuits diagonally in half. Dipping blades of scissors in boiling water, cut each marshmallow into four discs.

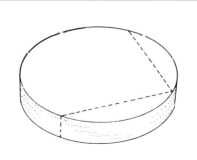

2 Set aside 20 marshmallow discs and, on remaining discs, cut one side to form a point, as shown.

3 Attach two full marshmallow discs to each wafer 'cone' using butter icing. Attach a pointed disc at the top.

4 Pipe 'drips of ice-cream' on 'cones' using butter icing in a paper piping bag with the tip cut off.

Melody Maker

To celebrate a musician's birthday – a cake decorated with intricately piped musical instruments.

Ingredients
1 × 200 mm (8 inch) square cake
750 g (1½ lb) cream sugarpaste (page 14)
brown, orange and yellow food colourings
for airbrushing
brown and cream royal icing (page 14)
cream modelling paste (page 15)

Materials and Decorations
1 × 250 mm (10 inch) square cake board
1 × 300 mm (12 inch) square cake board
300 mm (12 inch) paper square, with 200 mm
(8 inch) square cut out of the centre
140 mm (5½ inch) paper square
160 mm (6½ inch) square paper frame,
10 mm (½ inch) wide
200 mm (8 inch) square paper frame,
20 mm (¾ inch) wide
airbrush
patterns for instruments (page 76)
tubes: Nos. 1, 2 and 3, and fine tooth star
waxed paper
brown ribbon

1 Stick the 250 mm (10 inch) square cake board centrally on top of the 300 mm (12 inch) square cake board.

2 Position the cake centrally on the 250 mm (10 inch) board and cover the cake with cream sugarpaste.

3 Place the 300 mm (12 inch) paper square over the top of the cake and position the 140 mm (5½ inch) paper square and the 160 mm (6½ inch) square paper frame in the centre. Making sure that the pieces of paper do not move, spray the area surrounding the central square and frame with an airbrush using brown colouring.

4 Remove the 160 mm (6½ inch) square paper frame and replace it with the 200 mm (8 inch) square paper frame. Spray the area surrounding the central square with orange colouring, making sure that the pieces of paper do not move.

5 Using the patterns, pipe the violin, bow and four harps on to waxed paper with a No. 1 tube and brown royal icing, changing to a No. 2 tube to pipe the upright section and foot of the harp. Leave to dry.

6 When the instruments are dry, turn them over and pipe over all the lines except the strings and upright with a No. 1 tube and brown royal icing.

7 Roll out some cream modelling paste and cut out four 90 × 50 mm (3¾ × 2 inch) rectangles. Using the pattern provided, transfer the violin design on to all the rectangles. Curl two diagonally opposite corners of each rectangle, as shown. Leave to dry.

8 Pipe over the violin designs on the rectangles with a No. 1 tube and brown royal icing, piping the violin bow separately on to waxed paper.

9 Spray the four rectangles with an airbrush using yellow and orange food colourings and attach the violin bows with royal icing.

10 Using a No. 3 tube and brown royal icing, pipe a line around the inner central square on the top of the cake. Allow to dry.

11 Using a No. 2 tube and brown royal icing, pipe a line on top of the first line and, when that is dry, pipe another line on top using a No. 1 tube.

12 Using a No. 2 tube and brown royal icing, pipe a line around the outer central square. When this line is dry, pipe another on top of it with a No. 1 tube.

13 Flood (page 23) the borders of both cake boards with cream royal icing and allow to dry.

14 Stick brown ribbon around the edges of both boards.

15 Using a No. 2 tube and brown royal icing, pipe a snail's trail (page 20) around the base of the cake and around the edge of the top board.

16 Using a No. 3 tube and brown royal icing, pipe a snail's trail (page 20) at the base of the top board.

17 Using a fine tooth star tube and brown royal icing, pipe a shell border (page 22) around the edge of the bottom board.

18 Attach the rectangles to the sides of the cake with royal icing.

19 Carefully remove the violin and bow from the waxed paper. Using royal icing, attach them to the top of the cake, supporting them with pieces of sponge if necessary until the royal icing has dried.

20 Attach the harps to the corners of the cake, using a No. 1 tube and brown royal icing.

21 Finish by piping snail's trails (page 20) with a No. 1 tube where the harps meet the cake and along the base of each harp, as shown in the photograph.

'Have a Ball'

Treat the young football enthusiast to a goal-scoring cake and cookies with a bounce. Alternative patterns and appropriate colours can be used for other favourite sports.

The Cake

Ingredients
1 × 250 mm (10 inch) square cake
white, black and red butter icing (page 14)

Materials and Decorations
300 mm (12 inch) square cake board
cocktail sticks
5 paper piping bags
tubes No. 4 writing, Nos. 16 and 18 star

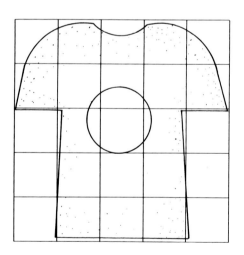

1 Trace T-shirt pattern and enlarge it to measure 250 mm (10 inches) at widest point. Trace football pattern and enlarge to measure 90 mm (3½ inches) in diameter. Cut out patterns.

2 Attach T-shirt pattern to cake surface with cocktail sticks. Carefully cut cake around pattern, keeping knife vertical.

3 Soften 30 g (1 oz) white butter icing and spread thinly over area where ball will be. Leave to set for several hours.

4 Prick holes through ball pattern where lines of ball markings meet. Place pattern on iced area and transfer markings by gently pricking cake through holes in pattern (use minimum pressure or icing will stick to pattern). Remove pattern.

5 Pipe all lines on ball using black butter icing and a No. 4 tube.

6 Use red icing and a No. 18 tube to pipe sleeve cuffs and neckband, moving the tube in a zigzag motion.

7 With white butter icing and a No. 18 tube pipe stars (page 21) over rest of T-shirt and sides of cake.

8 Pipe stars on white patches of ball using white butter icing and No. 16 tube.

9 With black butter icing and a No. 16 tube pipe stars on black patches of ball.

10 Should you wish to, pipe 'Have a ball on your birthday' around ball on T-shirt, using red icing and a No. 4 tube.

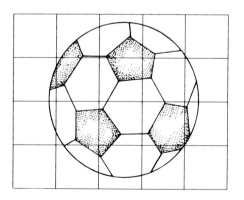

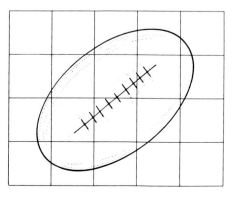

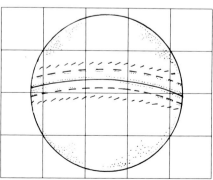

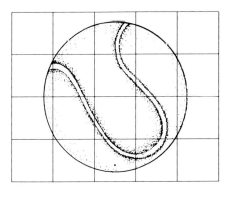

Patty Pan Cake Balls

Ingredients
10 cup cakes baked in rounded tins
butter icing in appropriate colours

Materials and Decorations
3 paper piping bags
tubes: Ateco No. 2 writing and No. 16 star

1 Turn cup cakes over so rounded surface is uppermost.

2 Football: With brown or black butter icing and No. 2 tube pipe lines of ball according to pattern. Pipe stars (page 21) on white and black patches of ball using a No. 16 tube.

3 Rugger and other balls: Spread softened icing in appropriate colour over cup cake. Pipe lines or laces with a No. 2 tube

Grand

Prix

A delightful cake for a Grand Prix racing fan.

Ingredients
1 × 200 mm (8 inch) square cake
750 g (1½ lb) white sugarpaste (page 14)
white and black modelling paste (page 15)
black, red and white royal icing (page 14)
neutral piping jelly

Materials and Decorations
1 × 250 mm (10 inch) square cake board
patterns for racing car and flag (page 73)
black and red food colouring
paintbrush
cotton wool
tubes: Nos. 1, 4 or 5

1 Cover the cake with white sugarpaste.

2 Trace the picture of the car on to the cake.

3 Roll out white modelling paste and cut out a 100 × 60 mm (4 × 2½ inch) rectangle for the large flag and two 25 × 35 mm (1 × 1¼ inch) rectangles for the small ones. Mark 25 mm (1 inch) squares on the large flag and 5 mm (¼ inch) squares on the small flags. Paint alternate squares with black food colouring.

4 Shape the large flag as shown on page 73 by propping it up with cotton wool until it is dry.

5 Roll black modelling paste to form the poles for the flags and set them aside to dry.

6 Outline the parts of the car with black, red and white royal icing. Flood the body of the car with royal icing or piping jelly, following the instructions on pages 23 and 26 respectively.

7 Mix black royal icing with neutral piping jelly and flood the wheels slightly unevenly to give them a bit of texture.

8 Flood the remaining parts of the car and when they are dry, paint the numbers on to the front of the car with red food colouring.

9 Attach the large flag and pole to the top of the cake with royal icing.

10 Pipe large beads (page 20) around the top and bottom edges of the cake with white royal icing in a No. 4 or 5 Ateco writing tube.

11 Using a No. 1 writing tube, add a dot of black royal icing to the beads around the base of the cake.

12 Attach the two small flags to the front of the cake.

A B C D E F G

H I J K L M N

Alphabet Cake

From Andrew to Zoe, there is an attractive alphabet cake for every birthday child. Number cakes for every age can be made in the same manner.

The Cake

Ingredients
1 × 300 × 225 mm (12 × 9 inch)
rectangular cake
brown, white and light orange butter icing
(page 14)

Materials and Decorations
350 × 250 mm (14 × 10 inch)
rectangular cake board
sharp, smooth-bladed knife
4 paper piping bags
tubes: No. 4 writing and No. 18 star

1 Trace and enlarge letter pattern to fit size of cake. Cut out pattern including inner sections.

2 Place cake on board and pin pattern to cake with cocktail sticks. Cut vertically into cake around pattern, taking care not to cut deeper than 20 mm (¾ inch) below cake surface. Do not cut out inner section (centre triangle of A). Remove pattern.

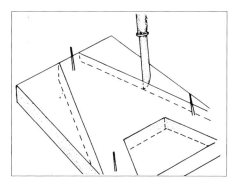

3 Starting at top left-hand corner, slice horizontally into cake at a depth of 20 mm (¾ inch) until you reach outline of letter. Remove this section of background. Repeat this process, cutting inwards from top right-hand corner, then from centre of base.

4 Spread softened brown butter icing thinly over inner sections to form background to letter. Lay pattern on cake and mark outline of inner section of letter with cocktail stick. Remove pattern.

5 Pipe outline around surface of letter with brown butter icing and a No. 4 tube. Pipe diagonal lines, 40 mm (1¾ inches) apart, across surface and sides of letter.

6 Fill alternate bands between lines with white stars (page 21) piped with a No. 18 tube. Fill remaining bands with orange stars piped with a No. 18 tube.

7 Pipe stars over background and sides of cake with brown butter icing and a No. 18 tube.

Blackboard Biscuits

Ingredients
10 biscuits cut and baked in blackboard shape
(use template below)
brown and white royal icing (page 14)

Materials and Decorations
2 paper piping bags
tube: No. 1 writing

1 Outline and flood biscuits. Allow to set. Pipe name of child on to biscuit using white icing.

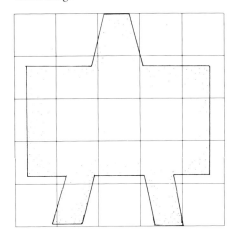

Dancing Shoes

Hand-moulded ballet shoes and pink, white and blue blossoms will delight a young ballet fan.

Ingredients
1 × 200 mm (8 inch) round cake
750 g (1½ lb) pale blue sugarpaste (page 14)
pink, blue, white and green modelling paste
(page 15)
pink and yellow royal icing (page 14)

Materials and Decorations
1 × 250 mm (10 inch) round cake board
small, medium and large flower cutters
ball tool
leaf cutter
tubes: Nos. 2 and 6
straight-edge cutter

1 Cover the cake with pale blue sugarpaste.

2 Hand mould a pair of ballet shoes from pink modelling paste.

3 Roll out pink, blue and white modelling paste and cut out a number of blossoms using the three flower cutters. Hollow each flower slightly with a ball tool.

4 Roll out green modelling paste and cut out a few leaves using the leaf cutter.

5 Pipe a curved shell border (page 22) around the top edge of the cake with pink royal icing in a No. 6 star tube and a snail's trail (page 20) around the base of the cake with a No. 2 writing tube.

6 Pipe a dot of yellow royal icing into the centre of each flower and attach a few small flowers and leaves to the side of the cake with royal icing.

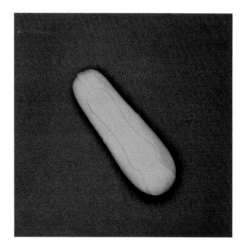

7 Attach one ballet shoe to the cake with royal icing.

8 Roll out pink modelling paste and cut out four ribbons with a straight-edge cutter. Immediately attach a ribbon to each side of the shoe and allow them to drape over the sides of the cake.

9 Position the second shoe and attach the ribbons in the same way.

10 Attach a small blue flower to the front of each shoe with royal icing.

11 Attach the flowers and leaves to the top of the cake with royal icing.

12 With a straight-edge cutter, cut out a narrow strip, long enough to go around the cake, from pink modelling paste. Twist the strip and position it on top of the snail's trail.

Kitten in a Basket

This delightful cake, accompanied by flower basket cup cakes and kitten lollies, will provide a delicious birthday spread.

The Cake

Ingredients
2 × 175 mm (7 inch) round cakes –
1 × 35 mm (1¼ inches) deep and
1 × 60 mm (2½ inches) deep
pink, white and brown butter icing (page 14)

Materials and Decorations
225 mm (9 inch) round cake board
2 wooden skewers or 2 long pieces of spaghetti
4 paper piping bags
tubes: No. 4 writing, No. 18 star and
No. 98 ribbon • cocktail stick
6 pieces of spaghetti, each 75 mm (3 inches) long

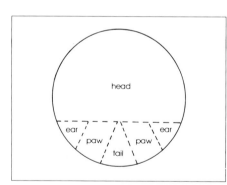

1 Place deep cake on board, and cut up shallow cake as illustrated.

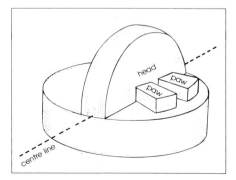

2 Attach head and paws to top of deep cake layer with butter icing.

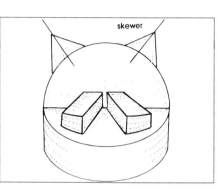

3 Attach ears to head using skewers or spaghetti for support, then soften a little pink butter icing with water and smooth on to fronts of ears.

4 Cover paws, back and sides of head and ears, and top of deep cake layer with white stars (page 21) using a No. 18 tube.

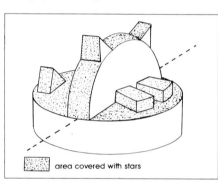

area covered with stars

5 Attach tail to cake with icing and cover with white stars.

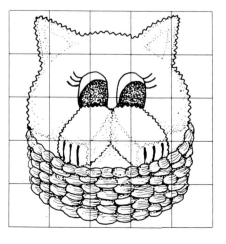

6 Soften a little white butter icing with boiling water and smooth across front of kitten's face to form whites of eyes. Mark in eyes with a cocktail stick. Pipe outline of eyes and centre with brown butter icing using a No. 4 tube.

7 Pipe white stars over remaining uncovered face and complete kitten by piping eyelashes and claws using brown butter icing and No. 4 tube.

8 Decorate sides of deep cake with pink basket weave (page 24), using a No. 98 tube. Finish rim of basket with a pink shell border (page 22), using a No. 18 tube.

9 Attach piped flowers (page 21) to cake as desired and insert three 75 mm (3 inch) lengths of spaghetti into each side of face.

Cup Cake Flower Baskets

Ingredients
10 cup cakes
100 g (3½ oz) modelling paste (page 15) in white and assorted colours
white and green butter icing (page 14)
royal icing (page 14) in assorted colours (piped flowers)

Materials and Decorations
3–4 paper piping bags
tube: No. 33 star

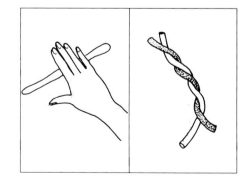

1 Make basket handles by rolling pieces of modelling paste into thin sausages about 125 mm (5 inches) long.

2 Twist pairs of different-coloured sausages together. Lie handles flat and curve them to

fit tops of cup cakes. Cut off excess length and leave handles to dry.

3 Attach dry handles to baskets with butter icing and decorate tops of cup cakes with leaves, piped with a V-cut piping bag, and piped flowers.

Kitten Lollies

Ingredients
10 lollipops
200 g (7 oz) marshmallow paste (page 15)
black food colouring

Materials and Decorations
modelling tool
fine paintbrush
1.5 metres (1½ yards) narrow, coloured ribbon

1 Make 20 mm (¾ inch) balls of marshmallow paste and press them on to the front of the lollipops.

2 Mould the paste around the edges of the lollies and smooth the surface.

3 Shape features with your fingers, starting each feature with a ball of paste. Attach by dampening slightly with water and pressing into position.

Horn of Plenty

With its basket weave horn and realistic moulded fruit, this cake makes an excellent centrepiece for a birthday buffet.

Ingredients
1 × 200 mm (8 inch) square cake
750 g (1½ lb) pale lemon sugarpaste (page 14)
light brown, green, red, yellow and orange modelling paste (page 15)
light brown and lemon royal icing (page 14)
yellow, green and brown food colourings

Materials and Decorations
1 × 250 mm (10 inch) square cake board
10 mm (½ inch) half-round crimper
waxed paper
tubes: No. 1 and small star
old-fashioned grater
pointed modelling tool
pattern for rose leaf (page 72)

1 Cover the cake with pale lemon sugarpaste.

2 Using a half-round crimper, crimp around the top edge of the cake.

3 Using light brown modelling paste and referring to the photograph for guidance, mould the horn and allow it to dry.

4 Place the horn on waxed paper and, using a small star tube and light brown royal icing, pipe basket weave (page 24) all over the horn, as shown. Leave to dry.

5 Using the photograph for reference, mould the modelling paste fruit and nuts. Three bananas, three small green apples, two large red apples, two oranges, one pear, a bunch of green grapes and three nuts are needed. Use the grater and modelling tool to shape and give texture to the fruit and nuts, adding details with food colourings.

6 Using the pattern and green modelling paste, mould two leaves and cut out three miniature stars for the strawberry calyxes.

7 Pipe the pips on the strawberries with a No. 1 tube and lemon royal icing.

8 Using a No. 1 tube and light brown royal icing, overpipe the crimping around the top edge of the cake and then pipe dots on the sides of the cake as shown in the photograph.

9 Using a small star tube and light brown royal icing, pipe a shell border (page 22) around the base of the cake.

10 Position the horn on the top of the cake and attach with royal icing.

11 Arrange the fruit and nuts as shown, and attach them to the cake with royal icing.

~~~~~~

Yellow Sports Car

Brighten up a birthday with this dashing car, biscuit road signs and tasty traffic lights.

The Cake

Ingredients
1 × 300 mm (12 inch) square cake, 50 mm (2 inches) deep
1 × 150 mm (6 inch) diameter round cake, 50 mm (2 inches) deep
pale blue, brown, yellow and white butter icing (page 14)

Materials and Decorations
350 × 250 mm (14 × 10 inch) cake board
5 paper piping bags
tubes: No. 4 writing, Nos. 16 and 18 star

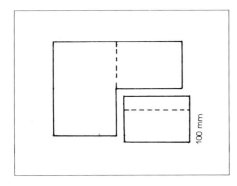

1 Cut 300 mm (12 inch) square cake in half, then cut one half to make two quarters. Cut one quarter (150 mm square, 6 inches square) to measure 150 × 100 mm (6 × 4 inches).

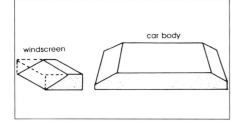

2 Cut front and back edges of half cake (300 × 150 mm, 12 × 6 inches) at an angle as shown. This forms body of car. Cut 150 × 100 mm (6 × 4 inch) piece at an angle to form windscreen.

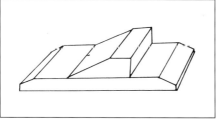

3 Attach windscreen to top of car body with butter icing.

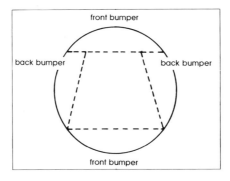

4 Cut round cake into front and back bumpers.

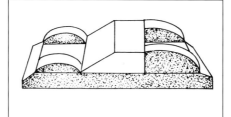

5 Attach bumpers to car with butter icing. Trim where necessary.

6 Cut 2 × 60 mm (2½ inch) diameter circles from remaining round cake. Split each circle in two to make four wheels and attach to car with butter icing.

7 Cut two small triangles from remaining cake to make front lights and attach with icing.

8 Spread softened, pale blue butter icing (use boiling water) on to windscreen and back and side windows. Spread softened brown butter icing on to wheels.

9 Outline windows, lights, radiator and doors with brown butter icing and a No. 4 tube.

10 Cover body of car with yellow stars (page 21), using a No. 18 tube, and pipe hub on each wheel.

11 Pipe brown stars with a No. 16 tube to form tyre treads, then pipe row of brown stars with No. 18 tube around base of car.

12 Pipe white stars using a No. 16 tube to make car headlights.

Traffic Lights

Ingredients
white marshmallow paste (page 15)
brown butter icing (page 14)
Smarties (or other coloured sweets):
red, orange, green
5 wafer biscuits

Materials and Decorations
1 paper piping bag
tube: No. 18 star

1 Roll ten white marshmallow paste balls, 25 mm (1 inch) in diameter, into 75 mm (3 inch) long sausages to form traffic light poles. Allow to dry.

2 Pipe three circles in brown butter icing, using a No. 18 tube, along the top third of the front of each pole. Press one red, orange and green Smartie into each circle centre to form traffic lights.

3 Cut five wafer biscuits in half. On to each half, pipe four circles of brown butter icing, one circle on top of the other, to form traffic light base. Gently push a pole into each base and allow to set.

Road Signs

Ingredients
10 biscuits, cut and baked in appropriate shapes
red, white and blue royal icing (page 14)

Materials and Decorations
2–3 paper piping bags
tube: No. 2 writing

1 Pipe details and outline and flood (page 23) each biscuit using desired colours.

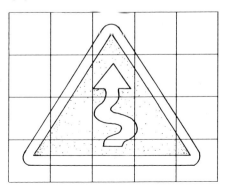

Chevrons

Ingredients
10 wafer biscuits
brown and yellow butter icing (page 14)

Materials and Decorations
2 paper piping bags
tube: No. 18 star

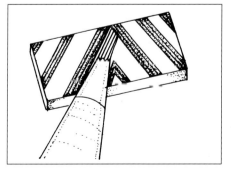

1 Pipe alternate brown and yellow stripes on to wafer biscuits, starting with yellow at centre of lower edge.

Winning Streak

The Cocoa Painting technique is used to create this cake for horse lovers of any age.

Ingredients
1 × 250 mm (10 inch) round cake
1 kg (2 lb) pale blue sugarpaste (page 14)
brown, dark and light blue modelling paste
(page 15)
blue royal icing (page 14)

Materials and Decorations
1 × 300 mm (12 inch) round cake board
pin
small plate
tracing paper
pattern for horse (page 75)
cocoa butter
cocoa powder
plastic artist's palette
cocktail stick
paintbrushes: Nos. 00000, 0, 1 and 2
hobby knife
plastic horseshoe mould
scalloped cutter
auger tool
tubes: Nos. 42 and 43
cotton wool

1 Cover the cake with pale blue sugarpaste.

2 With a pin, draw a circle in the centre of the top of the cake using a small plate to guide you.

3 Make a tracing of the horse and transfer it to the circle by going over the design with a sharp object.

4 Place a small marble-sized ball of cocoa butter into each of three hollows in an artist's palette and place the palette over a container of boiling water.

5 Add 5 ml (1 tsp) cocoa powder to the first hollow, less to the second and even less to the third. Stir the cocoa powder into the cocoa butter with a cocktail stick. You will have three shades of brown.

6 Using a fine paintbrush, paint the horse's head, beginning with the lightest shade. Deepen the effect by using the medium and darkest shades. Do not paint over the whole area; leave highlighted areas to create a more realistic effect. If you wish, use a hobby knife to remove small areas of the cocoa mixture to create further highlights. (Cocoa Painting page 28.)

7 Press brown modelling paste into a plastic horseshoe mould and cut away the excess with a knife. Lift the paste out with a pin and allow the horseshoes to dry on a flat surface.

8 Roll out dark and pale blue modelling paste and cut out two scalloped circles from the dark blue and one from the pale blue paste.

9 Flute the edges of the circles with an auger tool.

10 Cut a 10 mm (½ inch) wide strip from each shade of blue and cut a 'V' out of one end of each strip to form the ribbons. Allow the ribbons to dry on a flat surface. Attach the circles to each other and allow them to set.

11 Pipe a small shell border (page 22) around the centre circle and around the outer top edge of the cake with blue royal icing in a No. 42 star tube.

12 Pipe a shell border around the base of the cake with blue royal icing in a No. 43 star tube.

13 Attach the horseshoes to the cake with royal icing, supporting those on the top of the cake with cotton wool until the icing has dried.

14 Attach the ribbons and rosette to the top of the cake with royal icing.

Spaceship

Fresh from a voyage to the stars, this fantasy cake and its accompanying 'Men from Mars' will enchant the birthday child.

The Cake

Ingredients
225 mm (9 inch) round cake
3 large cup cakes
1 × 150 mm (6 inch) diameter (at widest surface) dome-shaped cake baked
in 75 mm (3 inch) deep bowl
very pale blue, dark blue and white butter icing
(page 14)

Materials and Decorations
325 mm (13 inch) round cake board
3 paper piping bags
tubes: No. 4 writing and No. 18 star
Smarties, red and brown
1 piece spaghetti, coloured with dark brown colouring

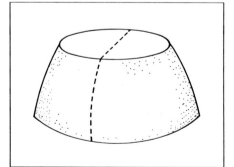

1 Place 225 mm (9 inch) round cake on board. Cut each cup cake in half and attach all six, evenly spaced, to round cake with icing.

2 Attach dome cake to round cake with icing.

3 Soften 155 g (5 oz) very pale blue butter icing with a little boiling water and spread evenly over entire dome.

4 Using dark blue butter icing and a No. 18 tube, pipe rows of stars (page 20) to form window frames on dome, starting at centre top.

5 Pipe squares and lines on each half cup cake with dark blue butter icing and a No. 4 tube.

6 Fill in squares on half cup cakes with dark blue stars piped with a No. 18 tube.

7 Cover remainder of spaceship, and outline windows on dome with stars using white butter icing and a No. 18 tube.

8 Add red and black Smartie 'lights' and break piece of spaghetti in half to form radar/aerials.

'Men from Mars'

You can create a variety of interesting outer space characters using the methods below.

Ingredients
10 lollipops
green, white, blue, purple, yellow and black
marshmallow paste (page 15)
black food colouring

Materials and Decorations
paintbrush
craft knife
modelling tool

Man from Mars 1 *(green and purple)*

1 Roll ball of marshmallow paste about size of large marble.

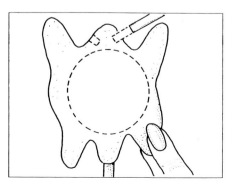

2 Press ball on to lollipop and shape with fingers, pulling out an ear on either side of face. Pull paste upwards to form top of head and downwards to form chin. Make a hole on each side of top of head.

3 Form two black marshmallow paste 'horns' and allow to dry. Dampen ends with water and insert in holes on head.

4 Paint on facial features with black food colouring.

Man from Mars 2 *(yellow, white and blue)*

1 Roll two sausages of marshmallow paste and make a ball on the end of each to form 'antennae'. Allow to dry.

2 Roll ball of marshmallow paste about size of large marble. Press on to lollipop and flatten into rectangular shape.

3 Turn lollipop face down and square off sides of head using craft knife.

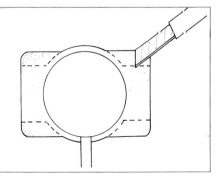

4 Roll two small balls of paste, flatten and hollow out to form ears. Dampen edges with water and attach to head.

5 Make two small holes in top of head using modelling tool.

6 Dampen base of dry 'antennae' with a little water and insert in holes. Paint on eye using black food colouring.

Mister Mouse

Add a touch of cartoon fun to the birthday feast with this bright mouse cake and a batch of tasty toadstool biscuits, cheese cookies and mouse lollies.

The Cake

Ingredients
1 × 300 × 225 mm (12 × 9 inch)
rectangular cake
beige, brown, pink, yellow and white butter
icing (page 14)

Materials and Decorations
350 × 275 mm (14 × 11 inch) cake board
cocktail sticks
6 paper piping bags
tubes: No. 4 writing and No. 18 star
3 lengths spaghetti, coloured with dark brown
food colouring

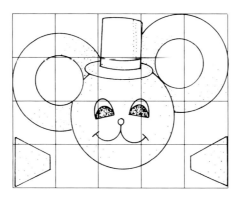

1 Trace pattern and enlarge to fit on to cake. Cut out pattern.

2 Place cake on board and pin pattern to cake with cocktail sticks. Cut cake around pattern, then remove pattern. Attach bow tie.

3 Soften 250 g (8 oz) beige butter icing with 25 ml (5 tsp) boiling water. Spread thinly over top of cake. Allow to set.

4 Prick holes in paper pattern along lines of hat and features. Place pattern over set icing and transfer markings by gently pricking cake through holes in paper (use minimum pressure). Remove pattern.

5 Spread white butter icing over the area of the eyes. Pipe outline of eyes and centres with brown butter icing and a No. 4 tube.

6 With beige butter icing and a No. 18 tube pipe stars (page 21) on face and around ears. With pink icing and a No. 18 tube pipe stars in centre of ears.

7 Pipe nose and mouth using brown butter icing and a No. 4 tube.

8 With brown butter icing and a No. 18 tube pipe stars on hat. Pipe stars on hat band and bow tie (excluding polka dots) with yellow butter icing and a No. 18 tube. Pipe red polka dots on bow tie with a No. 18 tube.

9 Break three lengths of spaghetti in half and colour them by wiping them with a piece of cotton wool dipped in brown colouring. Insert them in cake as whiskers.

Mouse Family Lollipops

Ingredients
10 lollipops
flesh-coloured, pink, white, black, brown, red
and yellow marshmallow paste (page 15)

Materials and Decorations
board to roll paste on
plastic roller
craft knife
black food colouring
pink dusting powder
paintbrush

1 Follow instructions for modelling lollies (page 53), making faces in flesh colour.

2 Make ears using shaped balls of flesh-coloured and pink paste.

3 Use small flattened ovals of white paste for whites of eyes, and flattened balls of black paste for centres.

4 Roll tiny ball of black paste for nose.

5 Brush cheeks with pink dusting powder and paint on mouth and whiskers with black food colouring.

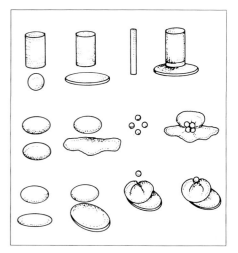

6 Using illustration as a guide, complete lollies by moulding hats, bows and ties and attaching to lollies.

Cheese Wedge Biscuits and Toadstool Mouse Houses

Ingredients
10 biscuits cut and baked as cheese wedges
(make template)
10 biscuits cut and baked in toadstool shape
(make template)
yellow, brown and red royal icing (page 14)

Materials and Decorations
3 paper piping bags
tube: No. 2 writing

1 Outline and flood biscuits. Add details.

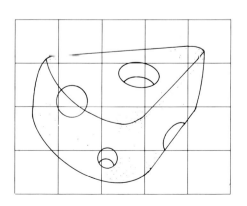

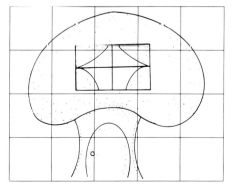

Clowning Around

This bright, happy clown is sure to be a success at a children's birthday party.

Ingredients
1 × 200 mm (8 inch) round cake
750 g (1½ lb) white sugarpaste (page 14)
red, green, yellow and flesh-coloured royal icing (page 14)

Materials and Decorations
1 × 275 mm (11 inch) round cake board
pattern for clown and balloons (page 74)
tracing paper
soft pencil
red and brown food colouring
fine paintbrush
tubes: Nos. 1 and 7

1 Cover the cake with white sugarpaste.

2 Trace the clown and balloons on to the top of the cake using either the Glass Stencil method (page 24) or by going over the back of the design with a soft pencil, positioning it on the cake and softly tracing over the picture.

3 Following the instructions for Floodwork on page 23, outline the design in the relevant colours, then flood the clown in sections, remembering to allow each section to dry before flooding an adjacent section.

4 Paint on the eyes and mouth with food colouring on a fine paintbrush.

5 Pipe small yellow dots with a No. 1 writing tube to finish off the edge of the frill, hat and trousers.

6 Pipe the balloon strings with green royal icing in a No. 1 writing tube.

7 Support the cake at an angle and trace the balloons on to the sides of the cake. Outline the balloons with green and red royal icing, then flood each balloon, following the instructions on page 23. Pipe on the balloon strings with green royal icing in a No. 1 writing tube.

8 Trace 'Happy birthday' and the child's name on to the top of the cake and pipe over the letters with green royal icing in a No. 1 writing tube.

9 Pipe alternate green and red shells (page 21) around the base of the cake with No. 7 star tubes.

Happy Birthday, Mother

The floodwork collar and red roses make this a cake any mother would be delighted to receive.

Ingredients
1 × 200 mm (8 inch) round cake
750 g (1½ lb) white sugarpaste (page 14)
white, red and pale green royal icing (page 14)
red and white modelling paste (page 15)

Materials and Decorations
1 × 275 mm (11 inch) round cake board
patterns for floodwork collar and embroidery
design (page 77), lettering (pages 78–79)
greaseproof paper
piece of glass
waxed paper
sticky tape
tubes: Nos. 0, 1, 2 and 3
moulded roses, half roses and buds (page 29)
non-toxic silver powder
little gin, vodka or caramel oil flavouring
silver ribbon bow (page 25)

1 Cover the cake with white sugarpaste.

2 Cut a greaseproof paper circle approximately 10 mm (½ inch) smaller all round than the cake board and draw the collar design on to it.

3 Place the collar design under a piece of glass and stick a square of waxed paper on top of the glass with sticky tape.

4 Outline the collar with a No. 1 writing tube and white royal icing. Now flood the collar, following the instructions for Floodwork on page 23, remembering to flood from alternate sides so that the icing flows together and does not leave join marks. Set it aside to dry thoroughly. It will take approximately 72 hours in warm weather.

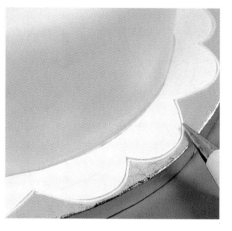

5 Cut out a second collar pattern, making it a few millimetres smaller than the first one and remove the centre circle, plus a few extra millimetres, so that the paper collar fits over the cake and slides down to the board.

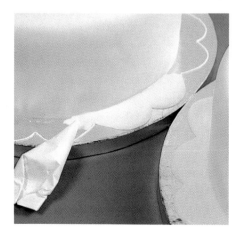

6 Pipe a line around the paper collar on the board with royal icing in a No. 1 writing tube. Remove the paper and flood the collar shape on the board as described above. Allow this to dry.

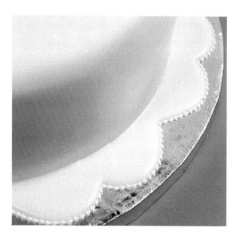

7 Pipe beading (page 20) around the edge of both collars with white royal icing in a No. 1 writing tube.

8 Pipe eight small roses with red royal icing following the instructions on page 30. Mould three large roses, three half roses and a bud from red modelling paste, following the instructions given on page 29.

9 Pipe the embroidery design on to both collars and on to the sides of the cake. Follow the design with the relevant colours in a No. 0 or 1 writing tube. Attach the small piped roses to the collars with royal icing.

10 Place the paper collar pattern on top of the cake and prick a circle on the cake approximately 2.5 mm (⅛ inch) larger than the centre circle.

11 Trace the word 'Mother' from an alphabet pattern on to a 50 × 100 mm (2 × 4 inch) piece of white modelling paste. Outline the letters with royal icing in a No. 1 writing tube and then flood them, following the instructions for Floodwork on page 29, and allow them to dry thoroughly.

12 Paint the letters silver by mixing the silver powder with a little alcohol or caramel oil flavouring. Attach the plaque to the cake with royal icing. Pipe a shell or beading border (page 20) around the plaque with a No. 2 writing tube.

13 Carefully remove the paper from the top collar by pulling the paper over the edge of the table while supporting the collar. Turn the collar around to release the other half.

14 Pipe a line of royal icing with a No. 3 writing tube, following the pinpricks to form a circle. Attach the collar to the cake by placing it on the royal icing circle.

15 With a No. 1 or 2 writing tube, pipe a small shell or beading border (page 20) between the cake and the collar to neaten the join.

16 Attach the spray of larger roses and rosebuds with a silver ribbon bow to the top of the cake.

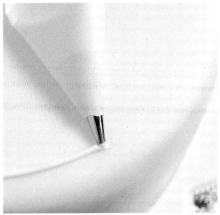

Ballerina

This graceful ballerina cake, with daisy and ballet shoe biscuits is sure to enchant the birthday girl.

The Cake

Ingredients
2 × 200 mm (8 inch) square cakes, both 40 mm (1¾ inches) deep
flesh-coloured, brown, white, pink and very pale blue butter icing (page 14)
piped flowers (page 30), if desired

Materials and Decorations
450 × 250 mm (18 × 10 inch) cake board
cocktail sticks
sharp, smooth-bladed knife
9 paper piping bags
tubes: Nos. 1 and 2 writing, Nos. 16 and 18 star

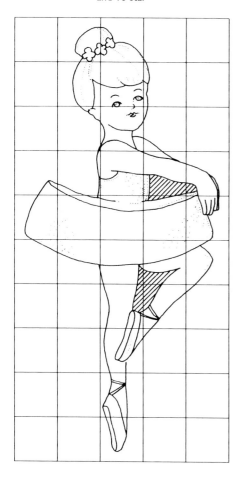

1 Trace pattern and enlarge to measure 325 mm (13 inches) from top of head to toe of shoe. Cut out, removing shaded triangles.

2 Place cakes on board and attach to each other and to board with butter icing.

3 Pin pattern to cake with cocktail sticks. Cut vertically into cake around outline of pattern, taking care not to cut deeper than 20 mm (¾ inch) below surface. Remove pattern.

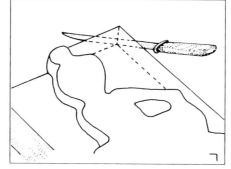

4 Start at a corner and slice horizontally into cake at a depth of 20 mm (¾ inches) until you reach cut outline of ballerina. Remove background cake from around ballerina. Repeat this process, cutting inwards from each corner, until all background is removed.

5 Soften 250 g (8 oz) flesh-coloured icing and spread over ballerina – surface and sides – but not on background. Leave to set.

6 Prick holes through pattern along lines of facial features. Place pattern on cake. Mark outline of cut-out triangles and mark facial features by gently pricking cake through holes in paper (use minimum pressure or icing will stick to pattern). Remove pattern.

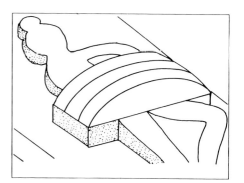

7 Cut three semi-circles from sections of cake removed from background to form ballerina's tutu. Sandwich these together with butter icing and attach to ballerina. Give the layers a slight upward curve.

8 Pipe outline and details of figure on surface of cut-out ballerina, using brown butter icing and a No. 2 tube. Pipe ballerina's hair with a No. 16 tube, and facial features with a No.1 tube.

9 Use white butter icing and a No. 16 tube to pipe stars (page 21) on bodice of dress, top (not edge) and underside of tutu. With a zigzag motion, pipe three rows of white 'frills' on edge of tutu, using a No. 18 tube.

10 Soften 30 g (1 oz) pink butter icing with boiling water and place in paper piping bag with tip cut off. Cover ballet shoes with icing. Pipe shoe ribbons using pink butter icing with a No. 2 tube. Pipe pink stars in ballerina's hair using a No. 16 tube.

11 Flood shaded triangles with softened pale blue icing in paper piping bag with tip cut off. Using a No. 18 tube, pipe pale blue stars over background and sides of cake.

Ballet Shoe Biscuits

Ingredients
10 pink sugar-coated almonds
10 white sugar-coated almonds
10 ginger nut biscuits
white and pink butter icing (page 14)
pink, white, blue and green royal icing (page 14)

Materials and Decorations
6 paper piping bags
tubes: No. 2 writing, No. 33 star and leaf tube

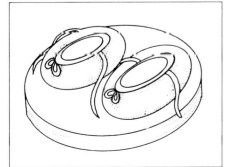

1 Soften white butter icing and spread on to five ginger nut biscuits. Spread pink butter icing on to the other five biscuits.

2 Attach two pink almonds to each white biscuit and two white almonds to each pink biscuit with butter icing.

3 Complete shoes by piping top rim of shoe, bow and ribbons with pink butter icing and a No. 2 tube.

4 Decorate with piped leaves and piped flowers (page 30).

Daisy Biscuits

Ingredients
10 biscuits, cut and baked in daisy shape (use cutter or template)
pink and white butter icing (page 14)

Materials and Decorations
2 paper piping bags
tube: No. 4 writing

1 Pipe outline of biscuits with pink butter icing. Pipe central dot in white butter icing.

A Basket of Flowers

The intricate piping around the edges of this attractive birthday cake complements the graceful basket on the top.

Ingredients
1 × 175 mm (7 inch) round cake
500 g (1 lb) white sugarpaste (page 14)
golden-yellow, pale green and white royal icing
(page 14)
pale pink, white and green modelling paste
(page 15)

Materials and Decorations
1 × 225 mm (9 inch) round cake board
pattern for basket (page 77)
tubes: Nos. 1 and 2, and medium star
flower cutters
leaf cutters
ball tool

1 Cover the cake with white sugarpaste.

2 Using the pattern, trace the basket on to the cake.

3 For the upper edge of the basket, use a No. 2 tube and golden-yellow royal icing. First pipe a short line of about 20 mm (¾ inch) along the centre of the top of the basket. Pipe a line on top of that measuring 35 mm (1¼ inches), and then subsequent lines one on top of the other measuring 40 mm (1¾ inches) and 60 mm (2½ inches). The base of the basket is also piped in this manner, starting with a short line and then two progressively longer lines over the top.

4 Using a No. 2 tube and golden-yellow royal icing, hold the paper cone at an angle of 45 ° and maintain a constant pressure as you pipe a 'comma' curving downwards, then to the left, finally flicking slightly to the right. Repeat as necessary to make the handle.

5 Using a No. 2 tube and golden-yellow royal icing, pipe the scalloped edge (page 20) of the basket, building it up with four or five lines of icing.

6 Pipe the main vertical lines of the basket with a No. 2 tube and golden-yellow icing. Pipe two lines on top of each other to form the sides of the basket, building higher towards the centre with three, four and five lines of icing.

7 Pipe two lines with a No. 2 tube over the length of the top of the basket.

8 Using a No. 1 tube and golden-yellow icing, pipe the trelliswork on the sides of the basket, using the photograph for guidance. Neaten the vertical lines by overpiping with a No. 1 tube.

9 With a No. 1 tube and pale green royal icing, pipe dots around the top edge of the cake at 10 mm (½ inch) intervals, as shown.

10 With a No. 1 tube and pale green royal icing, pipe loops from dot to dot.

11 With a No. 1 tube and pale green royal icing, pipe a teardrop with a curved teardrop on either side to form a *fleur-de-lis* in alternate spaces, as shown.

12 Using a medium star tube and white royal icing, pipe pull-up shells (page 22) around the base of the cake.

13 With a No. 1 tube and pale green royal icing, pipe loops at the base of the cake, using the photograph for reference.

14 Using flower and leaf cutters and a ball tool, mould the flowers and leaves from modelling paste, as shown.

15 Position the flowers in the basket, using the photograph for guidance, and attach them with royal icing.

Patterns

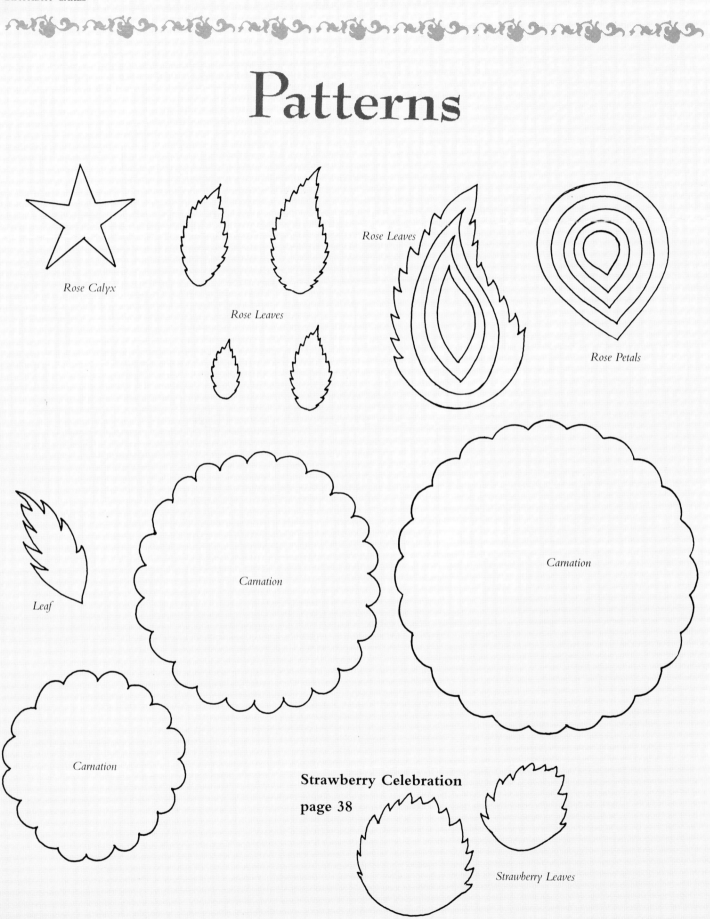

Rose Calyx

Rose Leaves

Rose Leaves

Rose Leaves

Rose Petals

Leaf

Carnation

Carnation

Carnation

Strawberry Celebration page 38

Strawberry Leaves

Grand Prix

page 46

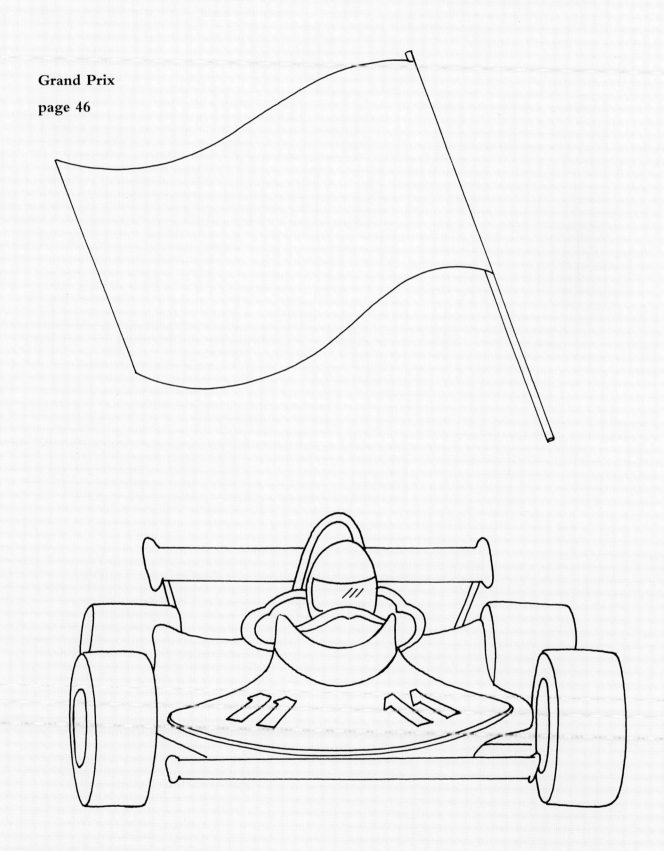

Clowning Around

page 64

Winning Streak

page 58

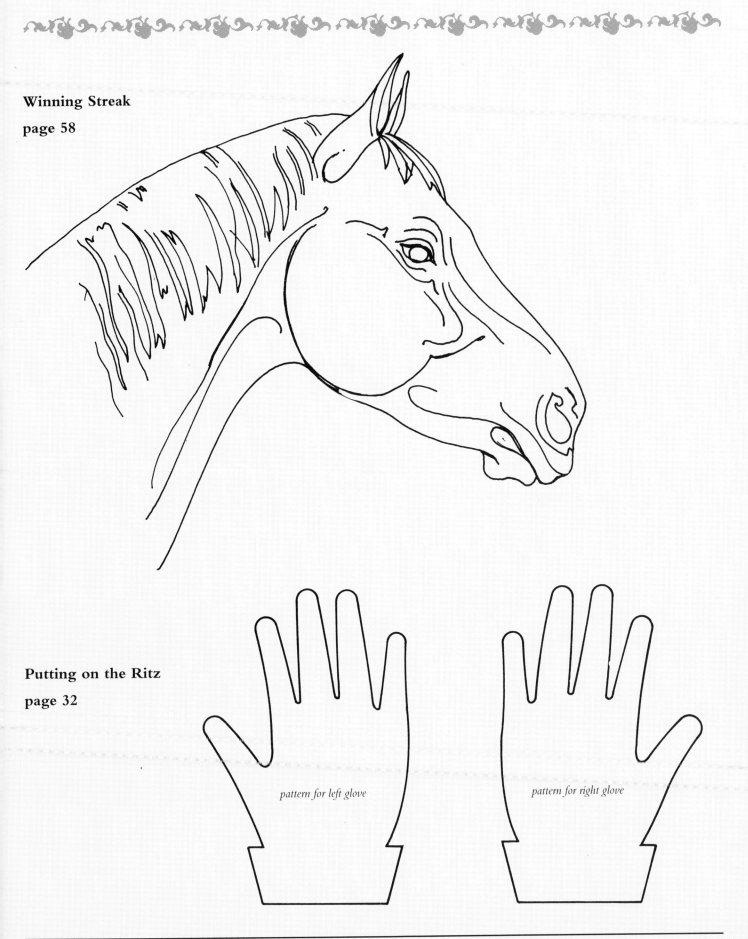

Putting on the Ritz

page 32

pattern for left glove

pattern for right glove

Melody Maker

page 42

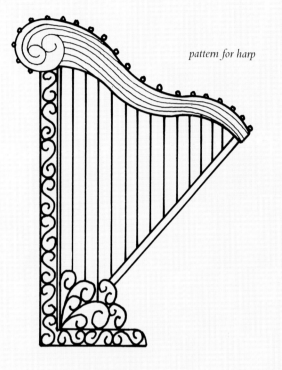

pattern for harp

pattern for design of plaque

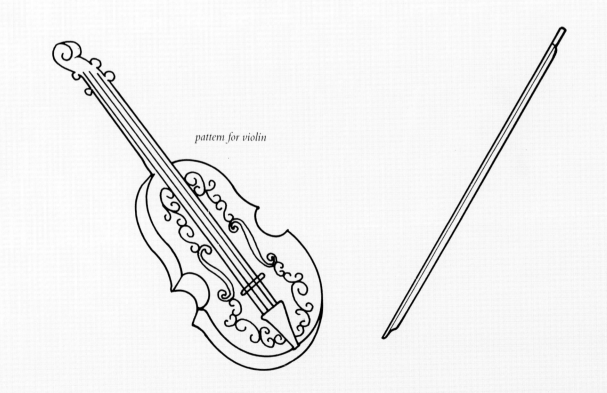

pattern for violin

Happy Birthday, Mother
page 66

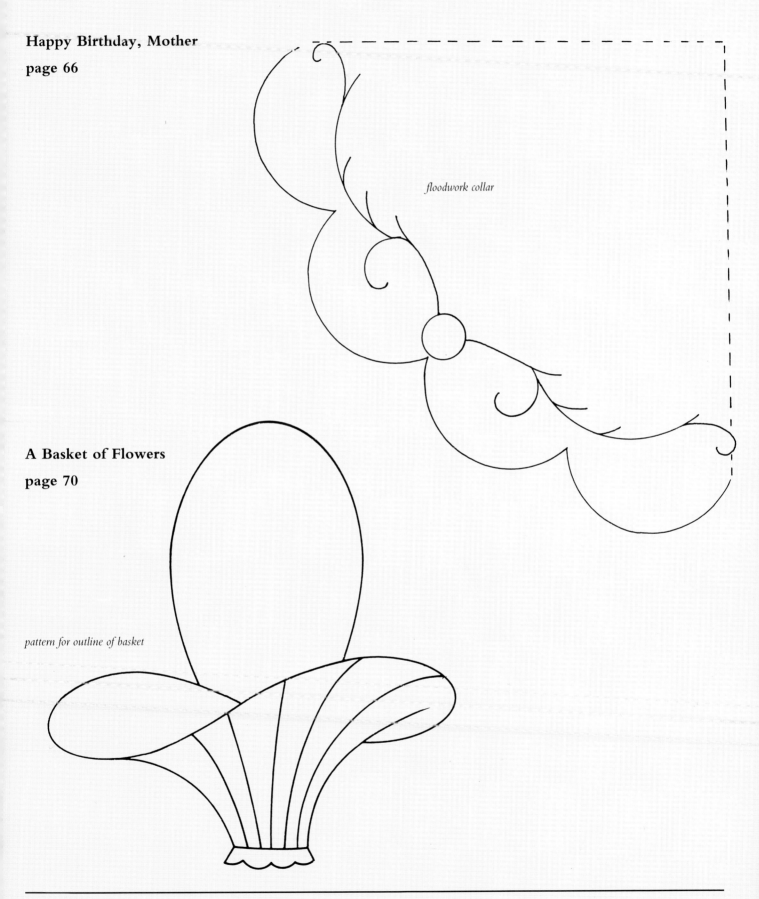

floodwork collar

A Basket of Flowers
page 70

pattern for outline of basket

A B C D E F G H I J
K L M N O P Q R S
T U V W X Y Z

abcdefghijklmn
opqrstuvwxyz
1234567890 &

ABCDEFGHIJKLMNOPQ
RSTUVWXYZ

Index